The Loving Someone Series

If your loved one has a psychological disorder, you want to do everything you can to help them feel loved, supported, and safe. However, it's also important for you to establish personal boundaries so that you can avoid becoming overwhelmed.

New Harbinger's *Loving Someone Series* was developed to help readers like you truly understand a loved one's disorder, the medication or treatments that are available, and how to take care of your own needs so that you don't lose yourself in the process. As the family member or partner of someone with mental illness, you face your own set of unique challenges. Our books can provide powerful, evidence-based tools to help both you and your loved one live happier, healthier lives.

For a complete list of books in this series,
visit **newharbinger.com**

"Nothing hurts more than losing your loved one to suicide. Nothing terrifies more than your loved one feeling or acting suicidal. Most people feel helpless, confused, and paralyzed—not knowing what to say, do, think, or feel. This precious book is an essential guide through the perilous storm, a treasure both for everyone who feels suicidal, and for everyone who loves them."

—**Allen Frances, MD**, professor and chair emeritus in the Duke University department of psychiatry

"'What do I do?' is the most frequently asked question I receive from family members, friends, and coworkers hoping to support and help someone they care about who has suicidal thoughts. Finally, there's a simple, easy-to-follow 'how-to' guide that can help anyone asking this question. Stacey Freedenthal's book fills a much-needed gap in suicide prevention and should be available in every mental health clinic, crisis center, and school. I'll be ordering in bulk to make sure I always have a copy on hand to share with those who need it."

—**Craig J. Bryan, PsyD, ABPP**, stress, trauma, and resilience professor of psychiatry and behavioral health at The Ohio State University College of Medicine; and author of *Rethinking Suicide: Why Prevention Fails, and How We Can Do Better*

"Stacey Freedenthal's book is an incredible journey into the lives of those who love people that think of suicide. The book helps all who read it ask the tough questions, manage guilt, and create a mental health plan before a tragedy strikes. It is a deep look into how people who have thoughts of suicide can find hope, light, and purpose, as well as all of the reasons to be here tomorrow."

—**Kevin Hines**, storyteller; award-winning filmmaker; and author of *Cracked, Not Broken: Surviving and Thriving After a Suicide Attempt*

"Stacey Freedenthal has done the impossible—combined scholarship with decades of personal and professional experience to write an easy-to-understand and endlessly helpful guide about supporting loved ones through one of the most confusing and complex human experiences—suicidal thoughts. Stacey gives her readers exactly what they want—answers and a path forward without resorting to platitudes and cliches. I will be recommending *Loving Someone with Suicidal Thoughts* to everyone."

—**Jonathan B. Singer, PhD, LCSW**, professor at Loyola University Chicago School of Social Work, past president of the American Association of Suicidology, and coauthor of *Suicide in Schools*

"*Loving Someone with Suicidal Thoughts* is a brilliant, beautifully written resource for all who support people struggling with suicidal thoughts. Stacey Freedenthal's clear, practical advice is a gift to family members, friends, and therapists seeking to understand and help loved ones with suicidal thoughts. Her empathy and expertise radiate throughout each page of this comprehensive, compassionate guide."

> —**Kathryn Gordon, PhD**, licensed clinical psychologist, and author of *The Suicidal Thoughts Workbook*

"Powerful, personal, professional, and unique. These are the first four words that sprung to mind when I read *Loving Someone with Suicidal Thoughts*. Genuinely, there is no book like this out there. Written by someone with decades of experience working in the field of suicide prevention, this book deals with all of the big questions around supporting a loved one who is suicidal. A must-read!"

> —**Rory O'Connor, PhD**, director of the Suicidal Behaviour Research Lab at the University of Glasgow, president of the International Association for Suicide Prevention, and author of *When It Is Darkest: Why People Die by Suicide and What We Can Do to Prevent It*

"Having lived in that 'dark place' for more than thirty-five years, I can confidently say that *Loving Someone with Suicidal Thoughts* gives you a clear-cut understanding of how to effectively help our loved ones who are in this dark place. I have a history of twenty-two suicide attempts, so having a book that helps describe the emotions that I've always wanted to share with the people who love me the most is phenomenal."

> —**Kevin Berthia**, suicide survivor and prevention advocate whose story of hope has touched diverse audiences around the world

Loving Someone

with

Suicidal Thoughts

WHAT FAMILY, FRIENDS, and PARTNERS CAN SAY and DO

STACEY FREEDENTHAL, PhD, LCSW

New Harbinger Publications, Inc.

Publisher's Note

This publication is designed to provide accurate and authoritative information in regard to the subject matter covered. It is sold with the understanding that the publisher is not engaged in rendering psychological, financial, legal, or other professional services. If expert assistance or counseling is needed, the services of a competent professional should be sought.

Unless otherwise noted, this book's examples of people with suicidal thoughts and their loved ones are fictitious.

NEW HARBINGER PUBLICATIONS is a registered trademark of New Harbinger Publications, Inc.

New Harbinger Publications is an employee-owned company.

Copyright © 2023 by Stacey Freedenthal
New Harbinger Publications, Inc.
5674 Shattuck Avenue
Oakland, CA 94609
www.newharbinger.com

All Rights Reserved

Cover design by Amy Daniel

Acquired by Jennye Garibaldi

Library of Congress Cataloging-in-Publication Data

Names: Freedenthal, Stacey, author.
Title: Loving someone with suicidal thoughts : what family, friends, and partners can say and do / Stacey Freedenthal, PhD, LCSW.
Description: Oakland, CA : New Harbinger Publications, [2023] | Series: The new harbinger loving someone series | Includes bibliographical references.
Identifiers: LCCN 2022037199 | ISBN 9781648480249 (trade paperback)
Subjects: LCSH: Suicidal behavior--Prevention. | Suicide--Prevention. | Suicidal behavior--Patients--Family relationships. | BISAC: SELF-HELP / Mood Disorders / Depression | FAMILY & RELATIONSHIPS / General
Classification: LCC RC569 .F717 2023 | DDC 362.28--dc23/eng/20221017
LC record available at https://lccn.loc.gov/2022037199

Printed in the United States of America

25   24   23

10   9   8   7   6   5   4   3   2   1   First Printing

This book is dedicated to my best teacher of all—
My mother, Beverly Freedenthal

Contents

Foreword   vii

Introduction   1

Chapter 1   Why Suicide?   9

Chapter 2   Your Loved One's Suicidality and You   25

Chapter 3   Managing Your Stress, Fear, and Guilt   37

Chapter 4   Asking Difficult Questions   63

Chapter 5   Brave Listening   79

Chapter 6   Getting Help   105

Chapter 7   Building Safety   125

Chapter 8   After a Suicide Attempt   135

Chapter 9   Coping with Conflict   151

Chapter 10   If You Feel Manipulated...   167

Chapter 11   Fostering Hope   181

Chapter 12   Recovery and Suicidal Thoughts   195

Acknowledgments   206

Resources   207

References   211

Foreword

There is no one in the field of suicidology quite like Dr. Stacey Freedenthal. She has uniquely positioned herself professionally and has an uncanny ability to connect with the larger public through her "Speaking of Suicide" website, social media contributions, and her spectacular writing—both scholarly and her larger media contributions. Notably, Dr. Freedenthal is a person with her own lived experience of suicidality and she has spoken bravely, and with tremendous candor and insight, about what it is like to struggle with suicide. Her voice from this perspective is often breathtaking in her abject honesty, courage, and transparency.

Objectively, Dr. Freedenthal is an accomplished scholar with an excellent record of peer-reviewed empirical publications. She is an award-winning teacher as an Associate Professor at the University of Denver Graduate School of Social Work. Dr. Freedenthal is also an accomplished clinical provider who speaks with clarity about clinical truths relevant to working with someone who wrestles with thoughts of suicide. However, these descriptive details do not begin to capture what is truly special about Dr. Freedenthal's perspective on suicide, particularly about the subjective nature of suicidal suffering. It is not hyperbole to say that no one in the field writes about suicide quite like she does.

Dr. Freedenthal began her professional career as a print journalist, and it shows, because she knows how to write and how to tell a story with elegance, truth, and power. I was a huge fan of her first book: *Helping the Suicidal Person: Tips and Techniques for Professionals.* This first book was a gift to clinical providers, offering a veritable treasure trove of ideas for any clinician who works with suicide risk. Her eighty-nine tips were informed by clinical science, superb therapeutic wisdom, and a practical clinical savvy that was richly illustrated by case examples.

In her new book, *Loving Someone with Suicidal Thoughts: What Family, Friends, and Partners Can Say and Do,* lay people are now the beneficiaries of Dr. Freedenthal's wisdom and multilayered perspective. Over the years I have met with countless families and friends who are tortured by fear and anxiety about what to do for the person they love who teeters on the edge of life. In the United States each year more than fifteen million adults and teens struggle with *serious thoughts of suicide;* this means many millions more people worry about those loved ones and often do not know what to say or how to say it before it is too late.

For these millions there is now this superb new resource. In the pages that follow, you will learn from Dr. Freedenthal everything you need to know about this tricky topic through her sensitivity, insight, compassion, and (nothing short of) grace. Dr. Freedenthal tackles this complex topic in her usual direct and sensible manner. Her ability to take the perspective of others is just astonishing. Each carefully crafted chapter walks the reader through practical and well-informed suggestions, with chapters addressing "Why Suicide," "Asking Difficult Questions," "Brave Listening," and "If You Feel Manipulated" to name a few. The useful ideas and essential truths imparted in this book are richly supported with case illustrations and specific language on how to best support a loved one who is suicidal.

Over my career I have met with countless suicide loss survivors who often feel deep regret about what they did or did not do to help a loved one lost to suicide. This feeling is pervasive among suicide loss survivors. To this end, when I meet with family, friends, or partners of someone alive but struggling, I directly encourage them to do all they can to minimize future regrets about what they did or did not do. I ask, "Ten years from now when you look back, will you be able to take some measure of comfort that you did everything humanly possible to support your loved one?" But now, when I have this conversation I will also direct them to the book in your hands as the best, most sensible, and most clear-eyed guide to loving and supporting a person who is suicidal. This book provides validation, comfort, wisdom, and valuable guidance on how to optimally proceed. Ultimately, this book will help decrease suffering and it will help save lives.

—David A. Jobes, PhD, ABPP, Professor of
Psychology, Director of the Suicide Prevention
Laboratory, The Catholic University of America,
Washington, DC

Introduction

If someone you love has suicidal thoughts—whether your teenage child, your partner, your friend, or anyone else you care about—I wrote this book for you. Yes, the person you love needs help, and hopefully, they're receiving plenty of it. But your loved one isn't the only one experiencing emotional pain, stress, and challenges. You need support, too.

The prospect of somebody you love dying by suicide is terrifying. All the "what-ifs" can keep you up at night and hijack your thoughts during the day. Almost fifty thousand people die by suicide every year in the United States—sons and daughters, mothers and fathers, husbands and wives, partners, siblings, and other family and friends. Suicide cuts lives short and creates unfathomable loss for those left behind. It's no wonder you're scared.

Your loved one's troubles can flood you not only with fear but also with other uncomfortable emotions like sadness, guilt, regret, anger, and more. You might agonize over what to say and what to do, how to help and how to cope. You desperately want your loved one to stay alive, and you also have your own life to live. There's just so much to navigate.

There's hope, too. You can learn how to talk with someone about their suicidal thoughts, how to listen in ways that help the person to open up rather than shut down, and how to assist the person in getting professional help, staying safe, and feeling hope. And you can better understand the ways your loved one's suicidal thoughts affect you, and ways to cope.

This book can serve as your own personal guide. I wrote it with you in mind because I know much of what you're going through. I come at this material from just about every possible angle of loving someone with suicidal thoughts: a therapist who helps suicidal clients; a parent of somebody who experienced suicidal thoughts; and a person who's attempted suicide.

Since 1995, I've dedicated my work to suicide prevention, first as a suicide hotline counselor, then as a social worker, researcher, and psychotherapist. My therapy practice specializes in counseling people with suicidal thoughts. I've also attended to countless worry-stricken parents, partners, and friends as they've fretted about their loved one's emotional state, struggled to keep the person safe, and muddled through their own painful feelings and circumstances.

Ten years ago, I created a website called Speaking of Suicide (https://www.speakingofsuicide.com). More than six million people from around the world have visited the site, and readers have left more than ten thousand comments. A great many of these comments come from people who love someone with suicidal thoughts. They ache to know both how to help the person and how to deal with their own feelings of helplessness, confusion, and sadness. My clients' and readers' experiences have taught me a tremendous amount about what family, friends, and others go through—and what helps—when someone they love considers suicide.

My expertise isn't only professional. Personally, I experienced the suicidal crises of my son when he was a teenager. My husband and I locked up our knives, razor blades, and medications in a digital safe in our bathroom, rushed our son to the emergency room more than once, and lived moment by moment with the wrenching fears of what we knew all too well could happen. During that time, I was writing the book *Helping the Suicidal Person: Tips and Techniques for Professionals* (Freedenthal 2018), yet I couldn't make my son's suicidal thoughts go away. I could, at least, use my knowledge to help him stay safe, walk him through creating a safety plan, connect him to professional helpers, teach him coping skills, and manage my own stress and fear. Now in his twenties, our son made it to the other side of those harrowing crises. He permitted me to share his experiences here in the hope it helps others to know.

Some of my insights come from my own struggles. Starting as an adolescent, I had urges to kill myself on and off over the years. In my twenties, I attempted suicide more than once. I've been doing better for a long time, thankfully, but my own lived experiences taught me first-hand the challenges that can beset people with suicidal thoughts—and their loved ones.

You can see that some personal experiences fuel my passion. Yet, while my personal journey has shaped my interests, this book isn't a personal account. Over the last twenty-five years, I've read countless articles and books about the challenges faced by suicidal people—and the people who love them. I've also witnessed these challenges, as well as recovery and growth, in my psychotherapy clients and their loved ones. This book's advice flows from the professional literature and my clinical practice.

If There's an Emergency Now

This book is intended to infuse you with knowledge you can use on your own. If you or the person you love are experiencing an emergency, please stop reading and get help now. If someone is in imminent danger of acting on suicidal thoughts or has already attempted suicide, do not leave the person alone, if possible. You have several options in an emergency:

- If you're in the United States, call 988 or 800-273-8255 (TALK)—both will take you to the 988 Suicide & Crisis Lifeline.

- Take the person yourself to the nearest emergency room if it's safe to do so.

- In urgent and dangerous situations, it may be necessary to call 911. (Chapter 6 gives cautionary advice on this.)

Those tips apply if your loved one needs help right away. What if you need help right now, too? A loved one's suicidal danger can trigger many painful feelings for you. If you have trouble getting through the day, meeting your obligations with work or family, or feeling hope or happiness, this book should be a supplement, not a replacement, for professional help. Especially if you are thinking of suicide, please get help from a therapist, psychiatrist, primary care physician, or other health professional. A trained professional can provide a space for you to vent, help you problem-solve, and in general, partner with you on this stressful journey. Whether or not you have suicidal thoughts, you can get help for yourself by calling the suicide prevention lifeline at 988 or 800-273-8255 (TALK).

What This Book Covers

Loving Someone with Suicidal Thoughts gives advice, support, and practical tools that you can start using right away. Quite a few books already address loving someone with a mental illness such as depression, bipolar disorder, or borderline personality disorder. Yet many people with suicidal thoughts don't have a mental illness, and the books about mental illness for family and friends usually devote little attention to suicidality.

The clear focus of *Loving Someone with Suicidal Thoughts* enables it to dig deeply into one of the biggest challenges you might ever face with someone you love. The book addresses the questions I encounter most often:

- Why do people turn to suicide?

- What are clues that someone might be in danger of acting on suicidal thoughts?

- How do I ask someone if they're thinking of suicide?

- What can I do to help someone stay safe?

- When should I call the police?

- What treatments are there for suicidality?

- What can I do to help after somebody attempts suicide?

- How do I persuade someone to get professional help?

- How do I tackle conflicts with someone who has suicidal thoughts when the last thing I want to do is create more stress?

- How can I deal with feeling sad, manipulated, fearful, angry, burned out, helpless, and more?

- How can I help the person feel and cope better?

- How can I help myself feel and cope better, too?

- Do people usually recover from suicidal thoughts?

Chapter 1 gives you a big-picture view of myths, facts, and biases about suicide. I've loosely arranged the rest of the chapters in chronological order, from start to finish of a suicidal crisis, but everyone's path is different. It won't hurt to read the book out of order, if you want to.

I wrote *Loving Someone with Suicidal Thoughts* for a diverse audience, from parents to partners, from family to friends. If you're concerned about a child, you should know the book mostly applies to adolescents and adults. Occasionally, you'll come across advice about children, like the guidance in chapter 8 on talking with youngsters about a family member's suicide attempt. This book's guidance can't be presumed to apply to children with suicidal thoughts because their needs and communication skills are so different.

Also, the book's advice might not apply if your loved one is dying of a terminal illness and lives where physicians can legally prescribe medicine to end one's life. Trying to prevent a loved one from ending their life in this context could create new strife and stress during your final days with the person. It's debatable whether such acts constitute suicide. In fact, in states with Death with Dignity laws, authorities are legally required *not* to classify physician-assisted deaths as suicide (Downie et al. 2022).

The book often uses the phrase "loved one" as a kind of shorthand for "the person you care about" or "the person you're worried about." It might help you, when you see "your loved one," to substitute the name of the person whose suicidal thoughts prompted you to read this book. You don't need to actually *love* the person. The book's recommendations apply whether you're in love, love someone in your family, love a friend platonically, used to love someone (like an ex), or just think the person you're concerned about is kind of cool. Love need not be felt to be enacted.

Taking Care While Reading

Suicide is literally a life-or-death issue, so *Loving Someone with Suicidal Thoughts* isn't light reading. Just as you'll find advice in these pages to take care of yourself while you support someone, I hope you'll also take care while reading. Here are some tips:

- Take breaks whenever you need to. Stop here and there to take in several deep breaths. You might want to put the book down for a while and do something for pleasant distraction, like take a brisk walk or watch a TV show.

- Read the book in the order that works best for you. You won't lose anything by skipping around.

- Talk with friends or family about what you read here. (And see chapter 3 if you feel the need to hide your loved one's suicidality from others.)

- Get professional help, if you can. Or get support in other ways, using the resources listed in the back of this book.

It's also a good idea to write in a journal or notebook as you read. Throughout the book, I ask questions for you to consider deeply. Writing will help you understand and work through your feelings. If you're not the type to journal, jotting down ideas on scratch paper or in your phone's notes app can help you process what's going through your head and heart.

Whatever approach you take, I hope you will embrace the book's overriding themes: there's a lot you can do to support your loved one, and you can honor your own needs, too. And I hope, as you immerse yourself in these pages, you'll feel less frightened, powerless, and alone in your journey.

It's difficult when someone you love has suicidal thoughts. You're about to learn many ways to better understand the person, cope with your own emotions, communicate, build safety, resolve conflicts, inspire hope, and take care of yourself. You can get through these stressful times. This book shows you how.

CHAPTER 1

Why Suicide?

Humans are endowed with a deeply ingrained instinct to stay alive. A hiker in Utah, trapped beneath a boulder for five days, sawed off his arm with a pocketknife to avoid dying (Ralston 2004). A man who fell the equivalent of twenty stories from a cliff in the Peruvian Andes crawled miles to safety, despite suffering from a badly broken leg, hypothermia, dehydration, and starvation (Simpson 1988). And it doesn't take a catastrophe for people's survival instinct to assert itself. Day by day, people look both ways before they cross the street, wash their hands to avoid infection, and take other life-saving measures.

Even so, some people's survival instinct appears to wither—or worse, it abandons them altogether. Their mind turns to suicide. Some carry out these thoughts. Every year, roughly eight hundred thousand people around the world end their own life. Many millions more try.

Why? This single, three-letter word torments many people who love someone with suicidal thoughts. Maybe it torments you, too. Maybe you want to shake your loved one by the shoulders and ask, "How can you want to die? Why isn't my love enough to make you want to live? Why can't you be happy, or at least at peace, with what you have in life?"

Or maybe you keenly understand how much the person suffers, and you grieve for them. Any way you look at it, it's painful, isn't it?

In this chapter, you'll look at what we know about suicidality. First, you'll read about the many different types of suicidal thoughts. Then you'll learn what makes people more likely—and less likely—to become suicidal. The chapter's last section looks at myths and facts about suicide and it invites you to challenge your own judgments.

Suicidal Thoughts

A desire to die or thoughts of purposefully ending one's life are considered suicidal thoughts. They're not rare. In a single year, roughly twelve million adults in the United States seriously consider ending their life and 1.4 million adults attempt suicide (Substance Abuse and Mental Health Services Administration 2020). Among high school students, almost 20 percent report seriously considering suicide in the prior year and 10 percent attempt suicide (Ivey-Stephenson et al. 2020).

The nature of suicidal thoughts can be dramatically different from person to person: a passing idea, an urge, a comforting fantasy, a disquieting obsession, a fully formed plan. Here are examples of what people experience:

I'm worthless. I don't deserve to live, even if I wanted to. People think I'm happy. On Instagram, I make it look like my life is great. But it's all fake. Nobody would like me if they really knew me. My parents and little sister will cry if I kill myself, but they'll get over it. In the long run, they're better off without me.—Monique, age fourteen

My brother-in-law killed himself five years ago. It devastated my sister and her four kids. Still does, years later. I would never want to put my worst enemy through what they've gone through, but in the last few weeks, I've had thoughts of killing myself. I don't want to. My brain just tells me, again and again, that suicide will solve my problems. I push these awful thoughts away, but they keep coming back. How do I make them stop?—Raúl, age forty-eight

I first thought of suicide when I was seven years old. My grandma died, and I wanted to go be in heaven with her. Now, I'm a physician, I have a wife I love and a nice house and the best cat in the world. But if something stressful happens, I think of killing myself. It's like an old friend. In a weird way, thinking of suicide calms me down. If I didn't know I could end things whenever I want, I'd feel trapped.—Yolanda, age 31

Obviously, there's no prototypical suicidal person. Everyone is unique, but people's thoughts of suicide usually reflect some mix of the following distinctions, to varying degrees:

Passive Versus Active

Many people don't want to be alive anymore, but they don't consider making that happen themselves. They wish circumstances, God, fate, or some other external force would end their life. They might make statements like these:

"I want to die."

"If only I could go to sleep and never wake up."

"God, please take me."

These are "passive" suicidal thoughts because they don't involve the person taking action to end their life. Compare that to active suicidal thoughts: "I want to kill myself" or "I'm going to end my life."

With Versus Without Intent

Without intent to act on suicidal thoughts, suicide is an idea, not a goal. Things become especially perilous when someone intends to carry out their suicidal thoughts within minutes or hours.

Sometimes, a person's suicidal intentions become clear only in tragic hindsight: the person updated their will, or gave away cherished belongings, or bought a pistol the week before their death. Most often, the only way to know if someone intends to act on suicidal thoughts is for the person to tell you; chapters 4 and 5 cover ways to make these conversations easier.

Fleeting Versus Obsessive

"Fleeting" thoughts last only a few seconds or minutes. They might come rarely or many times a day, but briefly. At the other extreme, suicidal thoughts can take on an obsessive quality, with suicide preoccupying the person much of the time.

Vague Versus Specific

Some people think of suicide very generally: "I want to kill myself." Others have specific, detailed thoughts about how, when, and where, what to do to prepare, who to say goodbyes to, and more. Generally speaking, the more obsessive and detailed suicidal thoughts are, the more dangerous. Not always, though. Some people think of suicide with great specificity but have little or no intent to carry out their plan. Conversely, some people attempt suicide without having planned it for more than a few minutes before acting (Paashaus et al. 2021).

Silent Versus Loud

People with auditory hallucinations can hear their thoughts as if someone else were talking to them. The voices people hear can command them to end their life. Some people recognize their hallucinations as a symptom of extreme stress or mental illness such as schizophrenia, bipolar disorder, or major depression with psychotic features, and they're not tempted to obey the voices. For others, their voices seem like truth-tellers, maybe even God. "Loud" suicidal thoughts are particularly dangerous in this context.

Intrusive Versus Welcome

Many people try to get rid of their suicidal thoughts, distract themselves, talk back, or disarm the thoughts of their power. They experience these thoughts as alien and frightening. Others, however, regard their suicidal thoughts as normal or even comforting, along the lines of the philosopher Friedrich Nietzsche's famous saying: "The thought of suicide is a great consolation; by means of it one gets successfully through many a dark night" (Nietzsche 2012, 84).

Crisis Versus Chronic

Books, movies, and news stories often portray suicidal danger as time-limited, like a hurricane. The thoughts are disruptive, intense, and extraordinary. It's an emergency. The person gets help and suicidal thoughts depart with the storm. For other people, suicidal thoughts are more like the constant drizzle of a rainforest. The thoughts last for many months or years without interruption. Or they might stop but start anew often, even for seemingly minor reasons. A comedian named Frank King speaks, in all seriousness, of contemplating suicide when he's told his car needs repairs: "I have three choices: Get it fixed, get a new one, or I could just kill myself. I know, doesn't that sound absurd? But that thought actually pops into my head… It's always on the menu" (King 2017).

If someone you love has thought of suicide for a long time, you might get lulled into thinking there's no danger. Beware of complacency. Sometimes, chronic suicidal thoughts turn into an acute, life-threatening crisis.

Danger Signs

There's no way to know for sure who will—and who won't—act on their suicidal thoughts. Still, in many cases, there are signs that someone's potentially in danger:

- Talking or writing about suicide

- Using the internet to research suicide methods

- Making plans or preparations for suicide

- Rehearsing or attempting suicide

- Feeling hopeless, trapped, or a burden to others

- Using more drugs or alcohol than usual

- Withdrawing from others

- Showing intense agitation, anxiety, or anger

- Sleeping too much or too little

Complicating matters, many of these warning signs are also quite common in people with *no* suicidal thoughts. And some people with suicidal thoughts don't give off any clues.

What Causes Suicidal Thoughts?

Most people with suicidal thoughts are hurting (Verrocchio et al. 2016). They're experiencing stress, trauma, chronic physical pain, anguish, overwhelm, mental illness, or some other condition that, to them, makes living feel unbearable. But that's not all. People with suicidal thoughts also tend to feel trapped. They experience a tunnel vision that focuses only on pain and problems. Has excruciating physical pain ever incapacitated you? If so, it's likely that all you could think of was how much you hurt, where you hurt, and how to stop hurting. Now imagine you felt certain the agony would never end. Might you want to die?

Not everyone with suicidal thoughts, though, suffers inexorable mental or physical pain. Some people are engulfed by problems that seem insurmountable to them, like a prison sentence or homelessness. Or they might experience intrusive suicidal thoughts or images that they wish would go away, often as a symptom of obsessive-compulsive disorder, schizophrenia, or another condition. Other people with suicidal thoughts don't experience significant problems, pain, or illness, but they're also not happy. They don't find meaning in life and they don't want to endure its demands any longer.

The tormenting question remains: *Why suicide?* Many people who suffer emotional pain, entrapment, mental illness, and existential despair never have suicidal thoughts. There's a lot we don't know, but we do know of many characteristics—also called risk factors—linked to suicide, such as the following:

Psychological Risk Factors

Mental pain or stress	Numbness
Hopelessness	Impulsiveness
Humiliation	Perfectionism
Guilt or shame	Trauma
Self-hatred	Poor problem-solving skills

Mental Illness

Anorexia nervosa	Depression
Anxiety	Post-traumatic stress disorder
Bipolar disorder	Schizophrenia
Borderline personality disorder	Other mental illness

Substance Use

Alcoholism

Opioid misuse

Other substance use or addiction

Self-Harm

Previous suicide attempt

Non-suicidal self-injury

Exposure to Suicide

Family or friend died by suicide
or attempted suicide

Suicide in the community
(e.g., school, Native American
reservation)

Physical Risk Factors

Chronic illness

Physical pain or disability

Traumatic brain injury

Insomnia

Sleep deprivation

Intense agitation or restlessness

Social Risk Factors

Grief or bereavement

Conflicts with family or partner

Divorce or other ending to
a romantic relationship

Social isolation or disconnection

Target of oppression by others
(for example, due to transphobia)

Economic Risk Factors

Poverty

Debt

Homelessness

Unemployment

Legal Risk Factors

Recent arrest

Jail or prison time

Probation or parole

Demographic Risk Factors

Male

White or Native American

Middle or older age (except Native Americans, whose risk is highest when younger)

Access to a firearm

You might have grown alarmed reading those lists if many of the items apply to the person you're worried about. Keep in mind, someone could tick off all the boxes and not have suicidal thoughts. And no risk factor, by itself, is deadly. As an example, people with depression are eight times more likely than the average person to die by suicide, but roughly 98 percent of people with depression don't end their life (Bostwick and Pankratz 2000; Moitra et al. 2021). The average risk for suicide is so small—roughly 0.3 percent for one's entire life—that the overall danger remains low even when that risk is doubled or tripled (Holmstrand et al. 2015).

Myths About Suicide

In a world of information overload, many messages you hear about suicide simply are wrong. Look at the myths below and see if it surprises you that all of these are false.

Myth #1: Everyone who dies by suicide has a mental illness

Conditions such as depression certainly increase a person's risk for suicide. But many people who die by suicide are contending with other problems like a loss of a relationship, a recent criminal or legal problem, or homelessness (Stone et al. 2018). *Fact: Studies indicate that anywhere from 5 percent to 65 percent of people who die by suicide don't have a mental illness (Milner et al. 2013).*

Myth #2: Suicide is always preventable

It's heartbreaking, but the reality is we can't always stop someone from ending their life. There are no objective measures—no lab tests, no blood work, no lie detectors—that reveal suicidal intent. Even when we know someone has suicidal thoughts, we generally can't control another person's behavior, and no treatment can always prevent suicide. Sometimes, suicide happens after friends and family did everything in their power to prevent someone from taking their life. *Fact: Suicide is mostly or often preventable, but not always.*

Myth #3: Once someone decides to end their life, there's nothing you can do to stop them

No, suicide isn't always preventable, but it's also wrong to say you can't do *anything* to stop it from happening. Researchers tracked down 515 people who were stopped from jumping off the Golden Gate Bridge. Up to three decades later, only thirty-five of the people—fewer than 10 percent—had died by suicide (Seiden 1978). *Fact: There are many things you can do to help someone you love resist suicidal urges—enough to fill this book, in fact.*

Myth #4: Someone who makes plans for the future isn't truly suicidal

A hallmark of suicidality is ambivalence. People typically are torn between living and dying, and they can simultaneously make plans for both. *Fact: It's not uncommon for someone to die by suicide even after they've booked a vacation, ordered new clothes, scheduled a lunch date, or made other plans for the future.*

Myth #5: People who truly want to die don't talk about their suicidal thoughts

What a destructive myth this is. It creates a Catch-22: please, tell someone you're suicidal, but if you tell someone, that means you're not really suicidal. *Fact: Almost half of people who die by suicide revealed to someone beforehand they wanted to die (Pompili et al. 2016).*

Myth #6: Asking about suicide can trigger suicidal thoughts

You'll read more about this myth in chapter 4. Just know, for now, that extensive research confirms asking someone about suicidal thoughts doesn't plant the idea (DeCou and Schumann 2018).

Judgments About Suicide

Up till now, this chapter has reviewed facts about suicide. Now, you'll look at your beliefs. Nobody can objectively prove these subjective statements right or wrong. But, if unexamined, your judgments can do harm without your realizing it. Negative statements about suicide and suicidal individuals can foster secrecy when what you want most is for the person you love to tell you about their suicidal thoughts. Who wants to disclose something that's considered shameful? Negative judgments also can make it hard for you to empathize with someone who's hurting. Bias can create distress for you, as Natasha learned:

Natasha's grandfather died when she was twelve. Her parents said it was a heart attack, but she overheard her mother tell her father downstairs, "We can't let the priest know he killed himself, or he won't get a proper burial." Her father hissed, "I'm not about to tell anybody. Do you think I want people to know my father was a weakling?" Already hurting from the loss of her Pop-Pop, Natasha felt bewildered, but she knew not to say anything to her parents. Now, thirty years later, her teenage son has attempted suicide. She's too embarrassed to tell her family. It means he's weak, doesn't it? At least, that's what she learned from her parents.

Here are some common biases about suicide and suicidal individuals. Read over the list and see if you agree with any of them.

- Suicide's a choice.

- Suicide is never rational.

- Suicide is selfish.

- Suicide is a sin.

- People who die by suicide are weak or cowardly.

- People who survive a suicide attempt didn't truly want to die.

- A suicide attempt is a cry for attention.

If any of those statements resonate with you, you might be unaware of some facts that, perhaps, could affect your opinion. Here are those facts now so you can have a fuller picture:

"Suicide is a choice."

We can't control what thoughts come to us, only what we do about them. Sometimes that's hard, too. If you doubt me, consider the massive numbers of people struggling with addiction, obesity, obsessive-compulsive disorder, and other conditions they try repeatedly, without success, to control.

Even if somebody appears to choose suicide, nobody chooses the suffering, illness, despair, or other problems that can make them want to die. The novelist David Foster Wallace (1996) likened suicide to a person jumping out of a burning building rather than enduring the pain of being burned alive: "Falling to death becomes the slightly less terrible of two terrors." If someone sees their choices only as suffering endlessly or ending suffering, that's not much of a choice, is it? Of course, there actually might be other options. The firefighters might already be putting out the fire, outside the person's view. A stairway hidden by smoke might lead to safety. Police might soon rescue the person by helicopter. But, because of the suicidal mind's tunnel vision, other possibilities can become invisible.

"Suicide is never rational."

Some people argue that suicide makes sense when a person experiences intolerable suffering that shows no sign of abating as a result of mental illness, chronic physical pain, physical disability, or inhumane living conditions. Others argue that suicidal urges are always irrational, the product of a disturbed state of mind that can change with the benefit of treatment, support from friends and family, or time.

Rationality is inherently subjective. Conditions such as depression and extreme stress can trick people into believing things they would normally recognize as false. Some people are convinced their life will never improve, nobody cares if they live or die, and the only way to stop suffering is to die. And, like the person in a burning building who can't see the exits, they might be wrong. Their mind lies to them.

While individual beliefs about suicide vary, governments and societies around the world tend to be more consistent; most places treat suicide as irrational. The courts allow people to be committed to a mental institution against their will if they appear to be in immediate danger of suicide. In the United States and many other countries, health professionals are legally permitted—expected, even—to protect people from killing themselves.

"Suicide is selfish."

You might wonder how it could *not* be selfish to die by suicide, knowing the pain it bequeaths to others. Consider Kurt Cobain, the lead singer of Nirvana, who killed himself in 1994. In his suicide note to his wife Courtney Love, he exhorted her, "Please keep going Courtney, for Frances." Was it selfish of him to leave her to raise a young daughter without him? Should he have protected his daughter from the injury of growing up without her father? The answers aren't as clear-cut as you might think.

First, many people with suicidal thoughts view themselves as a burden to others. In his suicide note, Kurt Cobain also wrote that his young daughter's life "will be so much better without [him]." To him, that was a fact. This isn't to imply that people who want to end their life are selfless. The labels "selfless" and "selfish" just don't fit. When someone dies of heart disease or cancer, we don't call that selfish, even though those deaths also create pain for others. Suicidal thoughts, and the problems that fuel them, are often as involuntary as an impaired heart or a malignant tumor.

There's another sobering thought to consider. It's painful, and if you haven't thought of it already, it might hurt to read these words: some people with suicidal thoughts complain that *their* loved ones are selfish for expecting the person to stay alive and suffer, just to spare others from grief. I don't agree with this sentiment, but the accusation does show that selfishness is relative, depending on whose pain is being considered.

"Suicide is a sin."

If you believe suicide is a sin, it's what you believe. It might be helpful to know that many major religions, while condemning suicide in general, have made allowances over the years for people who aren't able to make rational, informed decisions. For example, in 1992, the Catholic Church issued a catechism stating, "Grave psychological disturbances, anguish or grave fear of hardship, suffering or torture can diminish the responsibility of the one committing suicide. We should not despair of the eternal salvation of persons who have taken their own lives" (Nos. 2282–2283; Doyle 2020).

"People who die by suicide are weak and cowardly."

Suicide is sometimes referred to pejoratively as "taking the easy way out." Again, there's no right or wrong to this opinion, but an argument could be made that it takes bravery to end one's own life. Overcoming the biologically programmed survival instinct doesn't come easily. However, telling a suicidal person that suicide is brave doesn't help matters either.

"People who survive a suicide attempt didn't truly want to die."

Sometimes this judgment is true, but not always. Take the example of Xavier, a nineteen-year-old who attempted suicide while his parents were out of town. After doctors revived him in the emergency department, his dad said, "He's not really suicidal. If he'd wanted to die, he would've taken more pills." It might have soothed Xavier's father to believe his son wasn't in real danger, but this belief also can ignore someone's pain, deter others from helping, and imply the person is lying or manipulative. The reality is—even people who unequivocally want to die can survive a suicide attempt.

"A suicide attempt is a cry for help or attention."

Some people do hurt themselves in what looks like a suicide attempt when really they're trying to get help from others. In a national survey, roughly one in four people who reported they'd attempted suicide the prior year endorsed, "My attempt was a cry for help. I did not intend to die" (Kessler et al. 2005). With three in four people who attempted suicide reporting they had some intent to die, it's wrong to assume everyone's attention-seeking. Besides, if the person is "only" crying out for help or attention, doesn't that mean they need it?

It's helpful to look at your own biases about suicide. Respond in your journal to the following questions:

- What's a negative judgment you have about suicide or people with suicidal thoughts?

- How can the judgment help you or the person you love?

- How can the judgment hurt you, the person you love, your relationship, or others (such as your children)?

- How could you prevent this judgment from doing harm? For example, you might decide to stay silent about it or to try to look at the situation differently.

Ask these questions about other negative judgments you have, too, related to suicide. You might continue to hold those biases after questioning them. That's fine. Just be aware of your biases and try to minimize the damage they can do.

Hopefully, this chapter has given you a better understanding of suicide and suicidal thoughts and helped you to examine your biases. Now, in the next chapter, let's look at the many ways your loved one's suicidality can affect you emotionally.

CHAPTER 2

Your Loved One's Suicidality and You

Suicidal thoughts reverberate. Your loved one's struggles can create struggles for you. When somebody's problems are so intense that they consider suicide, you might wonder how your needs could compare. It's all relative. Your own troubles don't magically disappear just because someone appears to have it worse than you. In other words, you hurt, too.

This chapter addresses the painful feelings you might experience and the next chapter covers ways to cope. This is hard, painful stuff. If what you're reading begins to feel overwhelming, take a break or skip to the next chapter. With that caveat, let's look at some of the common reactions people have to a loved one's suicidality.

Sadness

The sadness of knowing your loved one thinks of ending their life can take your breath away. Jayla, forty-nine, explains many of the reasons why:

I cry all the time now. Because my son wants to kill himself. Because he's tried twice. Because our lives have changed so much. Because he could die. Because I brought him into this world, and it shatters me that he wants to leave it.

The chance that someone could die by suicide is distressing enough. Added to that, suicidal thoughts almost always come in tandem with other problems such as mental illness, substance use, trauma, stress, or loss. Whatever contributes to your loved one's suicidal thoughts may be another reason to grieve.

To better understand your own sorrows, write down in your journal your responses to the following questions:

- What saddens you about your loved one's situation?

- Are there others affected by your loved one's suicidality whose pain adds to your own? If so, what hurts your heart for them?

- How have you coped with your heartache?

Guilt

When it comes to things to feel guilty about, the sources are limitless. Maybe you deeply regret things you did (or didn't do) that you believe contribute to your loved one's problems. Maybe you feel guilty about not realizing the person was struggling, or how much. That's what happened to Victor, sixty-one, after his teenage daughter Izzy attempted suicide:

I can't stop going over in my head all the mistakes I've made with Izzy. I worked too long of hours. I lost patience and yelled at her about her messy room, her bad grades in school, her sassy attitude. I criticized her for being lazy and unmotivated when, I now realize, depression first overtook her. I wish I could take it all back. If she ends her life, I'll never forgive myself.

Do any regrets or mistakes haunt you? If so, respond to these questions in your journal:

- What do you feel guilty about in relation to your loved one with suicidal thoughts?

- How have you coped with your regrets and feelings of guilt?

Fear, Anxiety, and Worry

The unpredictability of suicide, along with the tendency of people to hide their suicidality, creates disturbing unknowns. If only you had telepathy! Instead, you can't know your loved one is thinking of suicide unless they tell somebody or take action, for example, by writing a suicide note or making an attempt. What if you don't know? The fear is never-ending for Onkar, twenty-three:

I'm afraid when my girlfriend talks about suicide, and I'm afraid when she doesn't because she might be hiding what she's thinking. I'm afraid when I think of all the things she could do to kill herself, and all the things I can't do to stop her. I'm afraid of all I know and all I don't know. Really, I'm never not afraid.

Take a look at your own fears. In your journal, answer these questions:

- What different aspects of your loved one's suicidality frighten you?

- How have you coped with your fears, anxiety, and worry?

Rejection

When someone wants to die, it can feel like they're rejecting you. After all, shouldn't you be worth staying alive for? Marisol, sixty-eight, asked herself those painful questions about her husband Alberto:

Al and I have been married forty years. He wrote a suicide note saying he doesn't have a reason to go on living. Don't I mean anything to him? I feel so abandoned.

Try to remember that people don't choose to have suicidal urges or the problems that lead up to them. Reminding yourself of these points can help you not take your loved one's suicidality personally. You might know this rationally, but still, feel hurt. In your journal, examine your experience by answering these questions:

- Does it hurt your feelings that your loved one considers suicide? Why or why not? (If your answer is no, writing about why you don't take your loved one's suicidal thoughts personally could fortify you later if your feelings change.)

- If yes, how do you cope with these hurt feelings?

Confusion

In some cases, everybody is astonished when someone reveals they're thinking of ending their life or attempts suicide. *She doesn't have any real problems. He always seems so happy.* These are common refrains, particularly when the person at risk is a perfectionist. Part of perfectionism, for many people, means hiding that they're having problems. Listen to Jake's experience:

I can't wrap my mind around it. My sister Christine has the perfect life. Makes good money. Has a partner and two boys who adore her.

But she attempted suicide last week. She couldn't have really wanted to die, could she?

Maybe you know your loved one is hurting and you're confused about how they can laugh and appear to have fun at times. The novelist Graham Greene (2015) wrote, "Life, however you lead it, contains moments of exhilaration... Even in danger and misery the pendulum swings." For many people with suicidal thoughts, good days—or, at least, good moments—can interrupt the flow of misery. And sometimes, this inconsistency can give you and your loved one whiplash.

If you feel confused by some aspect of your loved one's suicidal thoughts, answer these questions in your journal:

- What confuses you about your loved one's suicidality?

- How do you cope with your confusion?

Anger

The disruptions created by suicidal crises, the stress these generate, your loved one's refusal to make constructive changes—and more—can infuriate you. Chapters 9 and 10 address anger and conflict in depth. For now, answer these questions in your journal:

- Do you feel angry about your loved one's suicidal thoughts or behavior? Why or why not?

- If yes, how do you cope with your anger?

Embarrassment

You probably wouldn't feel embarrassed if your loved one had, say, leukemia instead of suicidal thoughts. But, as you saw in the previous chapter, cultural stereotypes condemn suicide—and by extension, suicidal thoughts and behaviors. Embarrassment can also stem from feeling you've failed the person in some way, or their suicidality reflects on you. Fatima's embarrassment stemmed from feeling she had failed as a mother:

> *My friends can't stop crowing about their kids' accomplishments. One friend's daughter got into med school and another's son is going to Yale. I don't know if my daughter Shakira will even survive, let alone go off to college. So, I don't tell anyone what we're going through. Even if they didn't say it, I know they'd think it's my fault she wants to die. That's what I believe, too.*

In your journal, examine your own feelings of embarrassment—or lack thereof:

- Do you feel embarrassed by your loved one's suicidality or fear others' judgments? Why or why not?

- If yes, how do you cope with your embarrassment or fear of judgment?

Hopelessness

Sometimes, you might feel hopeless, even though the situation isn't genuinely hopeless. Other times, you really can't see someone's situation improving. Seong, fifty-eight, was convinced his son Jung, thirty, could never get better:

> *Jung has schizophrenia. He lives on the streets and has no quality of life. This sounds terrible, but I'd completely understand if he killed himself. He's never going to get better.*

Your own loss of hope can lead you to feel resigned. You might forget that people in the most dire circumstances often can feel better, cope differently, or find meaning in life. In the example above, Seong's son started a medication, clozapine, that dramatically reduced his psychotic symptoms. He improved so much that he was able to go back to college and, after graduation, he got a job as an accountant. Jung still had auditory hallucinations, but he learned how to manage them better.

In your journal, answer these questions about feelings of hopelessness:

- Have you felt hopeless in relation to your loved one's suicidal thoughts? Why or why not? (Again, it can be therapeutic to write the reasons why you have hope, too.)

- If yes, how have you coped with feelings of hopelessness or helplessness?

Burnout

The phenomenon of burnout is aptly named: the flame of energy burns out, and darkness follows. This can happen when you don't have enough resources, support, time, or energy to care for yourself properly because you're caring so much for somebody else. Rafael explains how burnout looks for him:

I'm emotionally and physically exhausted. Almost every day, our daughter calls in some kind of crisis. We have to drop everything we're doing because what if we don't, and she kills herself? At the same time, I don't know if I can keep going on so little sleep and so much stress.

Are you burned out? Look at these symptoms and write down in your journal the ones you experience.

- I don't have enough time to myself.

- I can't go on like this; something needs to change.

- Nothing I do helps or helps enough.

- I'm overextended.

- I feel detached or distant from the person I try to help.

- I neglect my physical, emotional, and social needs.

- I'm more irritable than usual.

- I'm physically and mentally exhausted.

- I feel trapped.

- I use alcohol, drugs, or other unhealthy escapes to cope more than I used to.

- I feel cynical about my loved one, their problems, and my ability to help.

- I don't have any fun or pleasure anymore.

The more burnout symptoms you endorsed, the more worrisome the imbalance appears to be between meeting your needs and those of others. In the next chapter, you'll read about ways to manage stress and nourish yourself emotionally and physically.

Traumatic Stress

You might think of war, sexual violence, and other catastrophes when you hear the word "trauma," but a loved one's suicidal crisis can be traumatic, too. Isaiah's experience vividly shows how:

At first, I thought my husband had spilled a bucket of red paint on the bathroom floor. I know, that's absurd, but my mind just couldn't make sense of all the blood. Then I saw him lying beside the bathtub. He almost died. Now, it's been a month, but I keep reliving that night in my head. I close my eyes to sleep, and I see the blood. It's torture.

Reliving painful memories of your loved one's suicide attempt, fearing moment to moment the person will die by suicide, remaining hypervigilant for signs of danger, dreading what could happen—all of these can keep your mind and body in a constant state of alarm. These uncomfortable reactions usually subside, but if they persist, they can be signs of post-traumatic stress disorder (American Psychiatric Association 2022).

In your journal, respond to these questions about your own experiences:

- Have you felt traumatized by some aspect of your loved one's suicidality? If so, how?

- How have you coped with this trauma?

Depression

If you're experiencing significant sadness, guilt, hopelessness, and physical problems such as changes in energy, concentration, sleep, or appetite, it's possible you have depression (American Psychiatric Association 2022). An especially worrisome sign is suicidal thoughts. Depression isn't just a bad mood. It's a physical condition that affects thoughts, emotions, and physical functions, as Jackie's experience shows:

> *I'm so tired of stressing about my father that I don't get enjoyment out of anything anymore, not even my favorite foods. I feel down all the time. I don't have the flu or anything like that, but all I want to do is sleep. Sometimes I even wish I'd never wake up. I feel so guilty for feeling this way.*

If you think you might have depression, I urge you to talk with a physician, a therapist, or another helper. There are effective treatments. Psychotherapy or medication both can help, and the two combined are even more powerful (Kamenov et al. 2017).

If Suicide's Already Affected You

As painful as it is when someone you love has suicidal thoughts, it can be more challenging if suicide has already touched you in some way. As Siobhan shares:

> *It takes me back. When my daughter tells me, "I want to die," I'm in seventh grade again. I'm leaving for school. My mom's lying on the sofa by the front door. She says to me, "When you get home from school, I'll be dead. I'm going to kill myself." She's told me this before, more than once. I figure she's being a drama queen. But when I get home from school that day, I find her body. How can I not freak out when my daughter talks about suicide?*

Maybe, like Siobhan, you've had someone close to you die by suicide or you grew up with a family member who often was suicidal. Maybe you yourself had suicidal thoughts in the past. Maybe you have them now.

Whatever the case, your own experiences can shape your reactions—for better and for worse. On the one hand, your lived experience might give you insights that help you to understand, feel compassion, and listen with empathy to your loved one. Yet, their pain might revive memories and pain about your own suicidality.

Also, your own experiences can mislead you. If you once had suicidal thoughts and recovered, you might minimize the danger someone is in. Conversely, if you've lost somebody you love to suicide, you might live with such debilitating fear of reliving that loss that you overreact.

If you've had experiences in the past with a loved one's suicidal thoughts, your own suicidal thoughts, or suicide loss, explore these questions in your journal:

- In the past, how has someone else's suicidality affected you?

- What experiences have you personally had with thinking of suicide or attempting suicide?

- How might your past experiences negatively affect your efforts to help your loved one now? For example, how might they cause you to underreact or overreact to your loved one's suicidality?

- How might your past experiences positively affect your ability to help your loved one now?

This chapter covered a lot of heavy emotions that can emerge when someone you love has suicidal thoughts. Don't worry—I don't intend to stress you out and strand you with those feelings. The next chapter addresses various strategies for coping.

CHAPTER 3

Managing Your Stress, Fear, and Guilt

There's no way around it: it's often stressful, frightening, and painful when someone you love has suicidal thoughts. It's sort of like visiting Antarctica during the winter. You know it's going to be darn cold. You can't change that fact of life, but you can bundle up in warm clothes, socks, and boots to avoid freezing. Similarly, when you love someone who thinks of suicide, you can bundle yourself up with support, coping skills, self-care—and more.

In this chapter, we'll follow the story of Anita, whose fifteen-year-old son, Justin, attempted suicide a month ago. Anita says:

Last week, Justin didn't come home from school on time. For a full half hour, I was sure he'd killed himself. Just when I was about to call the police, he came home. He was fine, but I wasn't. My chest hurt. I had trouble breathing. I felt lightheaded. I thought I was having a heart attack. My husband's a pilot, so I couldn't call him. I called 911 and an ambulance took me to the hospital. They did all kinds of tests, and nothing was wrong with my heart.

The doctor in the emergency room asked me if I was under a lot of stress, and I kind of burst into tears and laughter at the same time. Am I under a lot of stress? Between watching over Justin, worrying about him, and doubting myself all the time, that's stressful enough. But I also work as a pharmacist downtown, have a husband who travels all the time for work, have two basset hounds that need walks every day, take Justin to appointments, and try to keep the house in some kind of order. Really, I'm more overwhelmed than I've ever been. The stress never ends.

The emergency room physician told Anita she'd had a panic attack and she recommended therapy. Anita took steps in therapy that, in my clinical practice, have helped many people cope when someone they love thinks of suicide. These steps can help you, too.

Balancing Privacy and Support

The first thing to consider is whether you're rallying all the help you need. The worries, risks, and responsibilities of supporting someone who's thinking of suicide are usually too big to bear alone. At Anita's first appointment, her new therapist, Dr. Pérez, asked how her family and friends were helping her. "Nobody has any idea what's going on," Anita told him. "It's private."

Are you hiding your loved one's situation—and your own? This privacy can come at a great cost. Secrecy deprives you of feeling connected to and supported by others. Secrecy also leaves you vulnerable to shame and fear of discovery. It's a heavy burden to conceal such an important part of your life.

Despite the disadvantages, you might have important reasons for not telling others. Perhaps you dread their negative judgments or clumsy advice. Perhaps the person you love insists you keep it private. In some professional and legal circumstances, there can be repercussions for your loved one if others know they have suicidal thoughts. The person might also be embarrassed because of the cultural stigma.

If you haven't done so already, have a heart-to-heart talk with your loved one about their fears, needs, and wants in relation to privacy. You might decide to tell others regardless, depending on your own needs. What you both decide will be unique to your relationship, situation, and more; there is no one-size-fits-all advice when it comes to whom to tell, or not. (By the way, I assume most people reading this book are adults. If you're a child or adolescent and a friend's thinking about suicide or made an attempt, *never* keep it secret. Even if you promised not to tell anyone, even if you fear angering the person, remember the saying, "Better a mad friend than a dead friend." Tell a trusted adult such as the person's parents, your own parents, a teacher, or someone else.)

If you do hide your loved one's situation—whether partly or completely—write in your journal your responses to the following questions.

- What, for you, are the pros and cons of confiding your stress about your loved one's suicidal thoughts to others?

- What are the pros and cons of *not* confiding in others? (This question can seem like it's just the reverse of the above, but the risks of telling often are different from the benefits of not telling.)

- Weighing these pros and cons against each other, what option appears to do the most harm to you, your loved one, or both of you? Which does the least?

- How do you want to proceed?

In Anita's case, Dr. Pérez walked Anita through an examination of the pros and cons of confiding in her best friend, Imani—and of continuing to keep her stress secret. Anita trusted that Imani would respond with compassion and also maybe help take the dogs for a walk from time to time. But their sons were both sophomores at the same high school. Anita worried Imani might tell her son, and then others at Justin's school could find out.

Dr. Pérez explored why Anita was so fearful of others' learning about her son's suicidality. Was she embarrassed? Was Justin? After the session, Anita talked with Justin about what he wanted, in terms of openness. It turned out he'd already told his friends at school, including Imani's son.

Ultimately, examining the pros and cons of secrecy and openness helped Anita to recognize what she was doing wasn't working. She needed support.

Creating Your Support Team

If you're open to telling others, people can help out emotionally and logistically. They can listen and help you problem-solve. Stay with you as you watch someone who's in a dangerous state of mind. Take care of the pets or kids if you have to rush to the hospital. Hold on to dangerous items that you don't want to keep in the house. As Anita discovered, you might find you're not alone in your struggle:

In a phone call one Saturday, Anita let Imani in on her family's crisis. Imani expressed empathy and asked how she could help. She also disclosed that her husband had suicidal thoughts several years ago. Anita and Imani commiserated about the stress of it all. The connection was such a relief that Anita called three more friends that afternoon and shared the situation with them.

Hopefully, you have various people you can turn to. If you can't think of anyone to ask for help, that's a lonely place to be. I wish you had support from others because this is a trying time. It's also possible you're overlooking potential supports.

Take a moment to identify everyone you can enlist to help you, your loved one, or your whole family. I recommend writing this down on a separate piece of paper that you can put on the fridge or somewhere else handy or keeping the information in your phone. Include contact information so it's easy to contact people in an emergency. Take care to include the following kinds of support:

- Other family members

- Friends

- Your loved one's friends and, if different from your own, family

- People from your church, synagogue, mosque, or other faith community

- Teachers, counselors, administrators, or others, if your teen has suicidal thoughts

- Neighbors and coworkers you trust

- Your loved one's therapist and other health care providers, if you're permitted to consult with them

You can also seek out a support group. Connecting with others who have "been there, done that" gives you the chance to learn from them, to vent, and to be understood. Unfortunately, in-person support groups for family, partners, and friends of people with suicidal thoughts are uncommon. If you live in the United States, the 988 Suicide & Crisis Lifeline may know of resources in your area.

Social media is a possible resource, too. You can check out private groups on Facebook—or start one yourself—for people who love someone with suicidal thoughts. A couple examples are the Families of Attempted Suicide Support Group and the Support Group for Parents of Suicidal Teens. Groups are constantly started and stopped on Facebook, so do a search there to see what's available.

Challenging Your Thoughts

Anita felt buoyed by her friends' compassionate responses to her family's situation. Still, there was one important person who judged Anita relentlessly. That person was Anita:

> *I can't stop thinking it's my fault Justin attempted suicide. I should've known what he was thinking. Been more alert. Gotten him help earlier. I'm a bad mother. And now I should handle everything better than I do. I'm such a mess. I can't do anything right.*

It's been said that many people have a prosecutor living inside their head but lack a defense attorney. Like Anita, you might blame your loved one's suicidality on mistakes you've made as a parent, partner, friend, or in another role. Or you might feel convinced the worst-case scenario will happen when you can't really know that right now.

Feelings and beliefs aren't facts, but we often treat them as such. This is the essence of cognitive behavioral therapy: Your thoughts influence your feelings and behaviors, and your thoughts can be wrong. In turn, challenging your thoughts often can ease distress, at least a little. This might sound obvious, but is it really? Generally, people attribute their sadness or anger to things that happen in their life, not to their *thoughts* about what happens, too. Dr. Pérez wanted Anita to recognize how her thoughts exacerbate her pain:

> *"Sometimes sadness and anxiety are inescapable," he told Anita. "The problem is when our self-criticism goes unchallenged, it makes the pain doubly worse. If your best friend had a child who attempted suicide, would you tell it's her fault and she's a bad mother?"*
>
> *"Absolutely not," Anita said.*
>
> *"Exactly, because you might get slugged," Dr. Pérez said. "It's terribly harsh. How does it affect your mood when you beat yourself up like that?"*

"Terrible," Anita said, her eyes welling with tears. *"But wouldn't I feel bad, anyway? I mean, my son attempted suicide and is still depressed. How could I feel positive about that?"*

Anita's question reflects a central misunderstanding about cognitive behavior therapy. CBT doesn't advocate thinking positively. Rather, it guides people to think realistically. A sad situation is still sad. Unrealistic positive thoughts will beget more misery because you know they aren't true. Using Anita's example, if she tells herself, *I'm a perfect mother,* her feel-good lie emboldens her mind to make the feel-bad lie even louder: *Don't be ridiculous. I'm a bad mother, and here's why…*

Thinking realistically means avoiding exaggeration, minimization, and errors in thinking, what therapists call "cognitive distortions." To help Anita recognize the extent of her own cognitive distortions, Dr. Pérez handed her this list, drawn mostly from the psychologist Judith Beck (2021):

All-or-nothing thinking. You tend to view yourself and other people in extremes—all good vs. all bad, perfection vs. failure, and always vs. never, as examples.

Catastrophizing (fortune-telling). You regard your dire predictions about the future as facts, without entertaining other possibilities.

Disqualifying the positive. You ignore evidence that contradicts your negative assessments of yourself, the future, or something else.

Emotional reasoning. You assume whatever you feel is true.

Labeling. You apply a label that condemns you or someone else globally, without taking into account other aspects of yourself or the other person.

Personalization. You blame yourself for things that aren't in your control.

"Should" and "must" statements. You have rigid, oft-impossible expectations for yourself or others.

Hindsight bias. You blame yourself for not foreseeing a traumatic event, based on information you have now but lacked before it happened (Norman et al. 2019).

Dr. Pérez asked Anita to break down the thoughts she'd described to him earlier and for each one to ask herself, "Is this a belief or a fact?" Anita acknowledged that each judgment was subjective, even though they felt indisputable. Dr. Pérez then guided her to identify the cognitive distortion that misled her. This is what Anita came up with:

It's my fault Justin attempted suicide. → Personalization

I should've known what he was thinking. → Should statements, mind-reading, hindsight bias

If I'd been alert and gotten him help earlier, he wouldn't have attempted suicide. → Fortune-telling

I'm a bad mother. → All-or-nothing thinking, labeling, disqualifying the positive, emotional reasoning

I'm such a mess. I can't do anything right. → Emotional reasoning, disqualifying the positive

Recognizing her cognitive distortions was meaningful to Anita because it allowed her to see how much weight she gave to thoughts without countering them. It also gave her the opportunity to try to change her habits of thinking because Dr. Pérez was right: her self-condemnations only made her feel worse.

Next, Dr. Pérez asked Anita to give the evidence that each thought was true and the evidence it wasn't completely true. For example, Anita questioned the thought: *I'm a bad mother.*

Evidence for: *I couldn't stop my son from hurting. I didn't even know he was thinking of killing himself. He attempted suicide.*

Evidence against: *I'm getting Justin help now. I listen to him—when he lets me. And when I do screw up, it doesn't negate everything else I've done well as a mother. I take care of Justin. I spend time with him and show him I love him. I make sure he has all the necessities. And I am working hard now to help him feel better, however I can.*

Now it's your turn. Think of something in relation to your loved one's suicidality that distresses you. For the purpose of this exercise, pick a thought that isn't 100 percent true. There are other steps you can take when a negative thought is factual, which I'll describe soon.

Using your journal, answer these questions from the psychologist Judith Beck (2021):

- What do you tell yourself about what you're experiencing?

- Is what you tell yourself a belief or a fact?

- How does it affect your mood to believe that about yourself?

- What is the evidence your thought is true?

- What is the evidence it's not true, or mostly not true?

Now, while thinking about your challenges supporting your loved one, imagine somebody you love—a child, a friend, your partner—were going through the same situation as you, with the same uncomfortable thoughts and feelings.

- What might you say to the person?

- Is it different from what you say to yourself? If so, why?

- What can you tell yourself moving forward when you have this distressing thought?

Once you find words that are soothing but realistic, write them down. You're creating "coping statements." Use these statements as mantras when you're troubled by stress, fear, self-blame, or other difficult emotions. Some people write their coping statements on sticky notes and put them where they can see them or keep a list in their phone to turn to when needed.

Here are some examples to illustrate, but your coping statements will work better for you if you choose or create something that especially resonates:

This feeling will pass.

That's a belief, not a fact.

Don't assume the worst.

I'll get through this.

I'm doing the best I can.

One day at a time.

I'm a work in progress.

In time, Anita recognized that Justin's suicidality wasn't the only thing breaking her heart. So were the things she told herself—until she learned to be her own defense attorney.

Those are some cognitive therapy tools—you might consider them mental "hacks"—to help you avoid making thinking errors that can lead to or worsen bad moods, depression, and anxiety. However, even if you challenge your thoughts, even if you recognize they're not entirely rational, they still might *feel* true. And, the reality is, sometimes painful judgments and predictions are correct. Here are some things you can do for thoughts that are impervious to your logic.

Change Your Focus, If You Can

For some thoughts, it's important to ask yourself not only, *Is this true?* Ask, too, *Is it helpful to focus on this?* For example, Anita found herself constantly thinking, *Justin could kill himself at any moment*. Sadly, he could. It's a fact. But pummeling herself with that possibility worsened her sense of panic.

If you tell yourself things about your loved one's situation that are sad but true, you can take several steps to soften the effects. Ask yourself, *How does it help me to keep telling myself this? How does it hurt me?* Answer both questions honestly in your journal. Consider whether you'd give the same worrisome warnings to someone else in the same situation. Dr. Pérez asked Anita whether she'd say to a friend every day, many times a day, "Your son could kill himself at any moment. He could be dying right now and you don't know it." Of course, the answer was no.

If your distressing thought is true, look at the function it serves. For example, "Justin could kill himself at any moment" is a very helpful thought to have if it reflects your misgivings about keeping a loaded firearm in the home. If the thought isn't helpful and you're able to let go of it or rebut it, by all means do.

One way to temper a worrisome thought is to think of alternative possibilities as well. Don't just go to the worst case. Anita made a deal with herself: She'd give equal time to the negative *and* positive possibilities. Every time she thought Justin could kill himself at any moment, she'd remind herself Justin also could get better, stop feeling suicidal, and live a long, healthy life.

Practice Acceptance

Sometimes, trying to stop yourself from thinking something can make your undesired thoughts stronger (Wang et al. 2020). If you've tried to change or challenge your thoughts without success, try accepting your thoughts and feelings as they are with mindful observation. Acceptance isn't resigning yourself to a bad situation or fate. It's also not trying to make yourself believe something false. Acceptance is letting yourself think and feel whatever comes, without resistance or attachment. That is, you don't try to change your thoughts and emotions and you also don't grant them too much importance. They're just thoughts.

> *Anita couldn't shake the thought she should've been able to prevent Justin's suicide attempt. She'd tried challenging the thought:* You couldn't read his mind. He didn't tell you what he was planning. You would've done something if you'd known. *Part of her recognized that her guilt was undeserved, but another part of her didn't get the memo. Like an incessant drumbeat, the thoughts kept resounding in her head:* It's my fault. I'm a bad mother. *Dr. Pérez recognized that Anita simply couldn't change these thoughts, so he taught her to defuse their power by mindfully observing them.*

You can watch your thoughts come and go, without giving them weight or accepting them as truth. Some writers call this being a "compassionate witness" to yourself (Ott 2004, 26). As a compassionate witness, you can step back and witness your thoughts and feelings, neutrally noting each one. For example, whenever Anita had the thought *It's my fault,* she practiced saying to herself, *There's self-blame,* or, *There's guilt.*

There are many metaphors you can use to practice mindfully observing your thoughts. See if any of these work for you:

- Your thoughts and feelings are individual cars of a train. You can stand beside the tracks and watch the cars of a train go by—or you can hop on the train and get carried away by it.

- Your thoughts are leaves in a stream. Watch them float by. Try not to reach into the water and grasp one. If you do hold on to one, let it go.

- Feelings are like ocean waves. It's futile to try to stop them, but you can learn to surf on top of them.

Stay curious. Withhold judgment, positive and negative, about your thoughts and feelings. To establish distance, you can try restating your thoughts by adding the words "I'm having the thought that" at the beginning. For example, Anita changed her statement from "I'm a bad mother" to "I'm having the thought that I'm a bad mother."

Try it out yourself. Identify a distressing thought and write it down in your journal. Then, neutrally restate it in your journal from the stance of an observer by writing the same statement but first prefacing it with the words "I'm having the thought that…" The statements feel different, don't they? The first statement is presented definitively as fact. In the second statement, there's room for it to not be true. Observing your thoughts this way can put distance between you and what you're thinking, allowing for some detachment.

However you practice acceptance, the gist is the same: Observe your thoughts and feelings without automatically believing them or trying to change them. This, in turn, can help disarm troubling thoughts and feelings of their power. It also can spare you the frustration of unsuccessful efforts to change your thoughts. If you like this approach, I recommend the workbook *Get Out of Your Mind and Into Your Life* by the psychologist Steven Hayes (2005).

Solve the Problem

Distressing thoughts aren't always distorted. Sometimes, the situation genuinely is distressing—you made a mistake, your loved one's getting worse, or you're exhausted. Those can be legitimate, correct impressions. If your thoughts aren't distorted, listen to them for next steps. There's a problem to solve.

If you made a mistake, what can you do to correct it? If your loved one's getting worse, what can you do to help the person get more help? If you're exhausted, how can you make time for rest? Sometimes, the problem has no real solution. If that's the case, you may need to work through your feelings of grief and, as I describe soon, treat yourself with compassion. In this way, you don't resist the pain that's unavoidable and your mind doesn't heap more on.

Recognize Your Limitations

One of the most painful aspects of knowing someone you love has suicidal thoughts is understanding you could lose the person. This is not a distorted thought. It's true that, statistically speaking, chances are very high your loved one will survive. That small possibility of your loved one's dying by suicide is terrifying and all too real. This terror can lead you to expect too much of yourself.

In Anita's case, she found herself feeling inadequate because she couldn't ascertain what Justin was thinking. She faulted herself for not anticipating his needs. She thought she should be able to get him to "snap out of it." Why couldn't he recognize all the goodness he had in his life and in himself? She believed she ought to be able to persuade him.

Expectations aren't necessarily bad or wrong. They set a standard to strive for. Expectations can become toxic when you expect yourself to always meet them and it's not possible to do so. Like Anita, you might expect yourself to fully protect the person you love, make the person happy, and solve their problems.

Do you have unrealistic standards for yourself? In your journal, write down all the ways you hold yourself to high standards for your loved one but fall short. For each expectation, ask yourself: *Is this a realistic expectation or is it a wish?* If you recognize some of your expectations are actually heartfelt wishes, how does it feel to make that distinction?

Next, I want you to consider something painful, but necessary: As much as you want to stop the person you love from dying by suicide, there's only so much you can control. Even if, for example, you stay with someone twenty-four hours a day, you can't protect the person while you go to the bathroom, sleep, or shower. Even if you stay alert for clues about suicidal danger, you can't read someone's mind.

Recognizing your limitations can be heartbreaking. It hurts to realize you can't guarantee your loved one won't end their life. Paradoxically, recognizing your limitations can also be liberating. By giving up superhuman standards, you can devote yourself to what you can control. There's still plenty you can do, but with realistic expectations. You do everything you can, but also know you can't do everything.

Understand Guilt

Self-blame, regret, and guilt are very common among loved ones of people with suicidal thoughts. These feelings are tricky. It can be hard to distinguish between blaming yourself unfairly and taking responsibility for a mistake.

It's possible you haven't done anything wrong beyond the normal slights and mistakes that humans, by virtue of being human, inevitably make. Maybe it wasn't a mistake, just something you did for good reasons that left your loved one feeling hurt. Maybe, for example, you said no to something your loved one wanted. These kinds of situations are tough because you still need to live your life even while worrying about someone else's staying alive.

Perhaps your guilt is, in fact, well-founded—perhaps you did hurt or disappoint your loved one in some avoidable way. Maybe you hurt the person without meaning to. Maybe, because of your own anger, fear, or pain, you meant to. If you could relive the situation, you would do it differently, right?

If you're harsh or unforgiving toward yourself, what you should do next depends on whether your guilty feelings are founded on fact. Writing about your feelings can provide some insight. Think specifically about something you regret in relation to your loved one. Ask yourself the following questions, some of which you've already used in a different context in earlier journal exercises, and write your responses in your journal:

- What do you feel guilty about?

- Are any cognitive distortions at work? For example, are you personalizing something out of your control, blaming yourself for not having information at the time that you have now, or ignoring evidence that refutes your self-condemnation?

- What's the evidence your guilt is deserved and you really did something wrong?

- What is the evidence your guilt's not actually deserved?

- Whatever you did or didn't do, whether it was intentional and truly hurtful or not, can you forgive yourself? Why or why not?

These are difficult questions. Depending on whether your guilt is based on a cognitive distortion or realistic, the answers might soothe you or accentuate your pain. Soothe you, because your self-blame is undeserved and your inner defense attorney has a new case to take on with gusto. Accentuate your pain, because you plead guilty to your inner prosecutor's charges against you. And both might be true—your self-blame is deserved in some ways, but not in others. Now, what should you do?

If you decide your guilt about something you said or did is justified, it can help both you and your loved one if you own it, apologize, and try to make amends. Be gentle with yourself in the process. You're human. Everybody screws up, loses their temper, says hurtful things, and misunderstands. We are all works in progress. Try to look at your mistakes forward instead of backward. That is, look at actions you regret only to inform what you can do—or try to do—from now on. It's hard, I know. But you can't change the past, and punishing yourself over it helps no one. What helps is learning, changing, and growing as a result of mistakes.

If your guilt and self-blame aren't truly deserved, you might wonder why you feel so much of it. In my clinical practice, I've observed that unfairly holding ourselves responsible for something, though painful, can protect us from the even more painful recognition of just how random life is. At any moment, anything awful can happen. Guilt often reflects an effort, usually unconscious, to feel in control of what's inherently uncontrollable. If you caused something to happen, you also can cause it not to happen again, right? The alternative: if you didn't cause something to happen, you are powerless to prevent it from happening again. The alternative is terrifying. No wonder our mind deceives us! Cognitive distortions protect us, if misguidedly.

Whether you truly did something wrong or not, hold in mind that suicidal forces are bigger than you. Many, many things beyond your control are involved, like mental illness and societal conditions. You alone can't create suicidal thoughts in someone—just as, sadly, you don't have the power to banish someone's suicidal thoughts, either. That we alone don't dictate whether someone becomes suicidal is both a comfort and a curse.

Aim for Self-Compassion

Anita made progress in therapy toward experiencing less distress and anxiety about Justin. She stopped accepting her self-criticisms as facts, balanced them out with evidence to the contrary, and learned to mindfully observe her thoughts to defuse them of their power. But she still hurt. Sometimes, the pain felt unbearable. And her pain didn't arise from cognitive distortions or unhealthy guilt. She hurt because her son hurt. She hurt because he wanted to die.

One way to cope with your pain is to respond with self-compassion. Be tender. Extend sympathy toward yourself.

To build a habit of self-compassion, use this exercise by the psychologist Kristin Neff (2011). It's called a self-compassion break.

Call to mind a situation in your life that troubles you. Let yourself feel the stress and emotional discomfort in your body.

As you observe that you're hurting, say to yourself, *This is a moment of suffering.* Or say something else that affirms your experience, like, *This really sucks,* or, *I'm hurting.* These statements allow you to stay present with your feelings, without resistance or judgment.

Now, for the second part of the self-compassion break, say to yourself: *Suffering is a part of life.* Recognizing the universality of suffering doesn't mean "get over it," "it's no big deal," or anything like that. On the contrary, your suffering connects you to others. It's part of being human. You can tell yourself:

I'm not alone.

Everyone hurts.

We're all doing the best we can.

Put your hands over your heart or touch yourself in some other way that feels loving. Feel the warmth of your hands on you.

Now, say or think: *May I be kind to myself.*

There are other possibilities, too:

May I give myself compassion.

May I accept myself as I am.

May I forgive myself.

You can also think about what you most wish someone would say to you right now, and say it to yourself.

Those are the steps of the self-compassion break. How did it feel to try it? Write about your thoughts and feelings in your journal. Could you believe your compassionate response and extend some gentleness toward yourself? Or, on the other hand, did the exercise feel fake and contrived? And if you couldn't believe it, could you observe your disbelief without judgment?

If the self-compassion break doesn't help, I hope you'll try again. This is true of all the exercises in this chapter. Nobody expects to get in shape by going to the gym only one time. It takes practice and repetition. To learn more, see the book *Self-Compassion: The Proven Power of Being Kind to Yourself* (Neff 2011).

You live inside your head 24/7. What you tell yourself matters. Defending yourself against your mind's indictments, relating differently to your thoughts, taking action based on your realistic assessments, and treating yourself with self-compassion are ways to nourish yourself emotionally. You can also nurture yourself physically by dialing down your body's reaction to stress.

Calming the Effects of Stress

When the stress of her son's suicidality overwhelmed Anita, her body sounded the alarm. Her heart raced and breathing became difficult. She also had difficulty sleeping. She constantly felt tension in her body—her jaw, especially, giving her headaches—and also muscles in her neck and shoulders. These were physical reactions to stress.

Generally speaking, stress mobilizes our energy and focus. If you're hiking in the woods and see a mountain lion ahead on the trail, your stress response might save your life. Likewise, the stress of your loved one's suicidal thoughts can pump you with energy and motivation to support the person, get help, and look out for their safety. But that same stress response takes a toll on the body when it goes on for a long time. It can feel like a mountain lion is chasing you when all you're doing is going grocery shopping or having a light conversation with your loved one. This ramped-up feeling, when incessant, can create problems.

How does the stress of your loved one's suicidality show itself physically? Write in your journal the physical and cognitive symptoms you've experienced, using this list as a starting point:

- Insomnia

- Sleeping too much

- Difficulty focusing or concentrating

- Loss of appetite

- Eating more than usual

- Forgetfulness

- Sugar or carb cravings

- Loss of energy

- Too much energy/restlessness

- Constant worrying

- Digestive problems (nausea, diarrhea, constipation)

- Headaches

- Muscle pain

- Irritability

- Frequent colds or viruses

- Teeth grinding/jaw pain

- Chest pain

- Shortness of breath

- Racing thoughts

- Heart palpitations

- Sexual dysfunction

You can't eliminate all the stress in your life, but you can calm your body's reaction to it, at least temporarily. This involves inducing the relaxation response. This physiological change slows down heart rate, lowers blood pressure, and decreases respirations (Benson and Proctor 2011). In short, the relaxation response gives your body a mini-vacation from stress. You can achieve the relaxation response in as little as twelve to fifteen minutes using tools such as meditation, deep breathing exercises, and progressive muscle relaxation. When you have even a short amount of time for yourself, you can close your eyes, listen, and calm the stress response in your mind and body. Here is some basic information about each.

Meditation

Generally speaking, meditation involves fixing your attention on only one thing and returning to that focus when your mind strays. You can focus on anything dynamic like, for example, a chant, a candle flame, or the feel of your body as you move in yoga. Most commonly, people who meditate stay attuned to their breath as it wafts in and out of their body.

A goal of meditation isn't to stay perfectly focused or to eliminate all thoughts. That's impossible. Strive instead to return to your focus more easily over time. When you inevitably become distracted, don't beat yourself up. You can tell yourself, *Oh, well,* or something nonjudgmental like, *My mind wandered.* Then go back to the intended focus.

Deep Breathing Exercises

You have many options when it comes to deep breathing exercises. The simplest method is to sit or lie down comfortably, breathe in slowly and exhale more slowly, and repeat for however long you've set aside to do this. Deep breathing exercises are themselves a form of meditation if you focus on the movement of your breath as it enters your body through your nose or mouth, travels past your chest to your belly, and then leaves through your nose or mouth.

Progressive Muscle Relaxation

This exercise involves tensing and relaxing small groups of muscles throughout your body, from your head to your toes, while also engaging in deep breathing. Some people do this in bed, right before going to sleep, but you can do it any time.

After her trip to the emergency room and before she started therapy, Anita had two more panic attacks. Each was an ordeal. She recalled the doctor's assurances that she wasn't having a heart attack, but the heart palpitations, difficulty breathing, lightheadedness, and extreme anxiety made her worry about her mental stability. Anita found a lot of value in the relaxation exercises:

In their first session together, Dr. Pérez instructed Anita on activating the relaxation response. Anita began meditating for fifteen minutes in the morning. Throughout the day, she'd be careful to breathe deeply whenever she felt short of breath. At night, she completed the progressive muscle relaxation exercise when she got into bed. Not only did her panic attacks go away but Anita also found she slept better and had more energy throughout the day.

These relaxation exercises are only a small sample. For more ways to combat the physical effects of stress, see *The Relaxation and Stress Reduction Workbook* (Davis et al. 2019). To learn more fully about meditation, the Buddhist monk Thich Nhat Hanh offers excellent instruction in his book *The Miracle of Mindfulness: An Introduction to the Practice of Meditation* (1987). There also are numerous websites and apps with instructions on mindfulness, meditation, deep breathing exercises, and progressive muscle relaxation.

Tending to Yourself

Do you take good care of yourself? When Dr. Pérez asked Anita that question, she again laughed and cried simultaneously. "I don't have the time," she said. "I'm too busy taking care of Justin—or worrying about him."

You've probably heard the phrase many times: "self-care." Nourish your body, mind, and soul. That sounds wonderful, doesn't it? When you're stressed or in crisis, it can seem like an impossible indulgence to get a good night's sleep, let alone to do something pleasurable just for you.

Your loved one's suicidal crisis can subject you to what one writer aptly labeled the "tyranny of the urgent" (Hummel 1994). You do what needs to get done, and little else. Yet, self-care is crucial when you're supporting someone with suicidal thoughts. How can you best support the person if you're exhausted, cranky, and burned out?

Dr. Pérez gave Anita a questionnaire to assess where she might be neglecting herself. She lamented, while completing it, that it'd been a month since she'd had the time and energy to take her morning jog and at least that long since she'd done anything pleasurable just for herself.

What can you do to build more rest, nourishment, exercise, pleasure, and other things into your life that are often viewed as extras, but are essential to help your loved one the best you can? You might have heard the saying, often attributed to the French author Antoine de Saint-Exupéry, "A goal without a plan is just a wish." If you want to attend better to your own needs, you need a plan.

A good self-care plan addresses your physical, emotional, spiritual, social, and professional well-being. When you're helping someone else in crisis or immersed in that crisis yourself, you can forget what you need to do for yourself. Consider your self-care plan a reminder.

It's good to start small. When setting goals or trying to adopt new habits, people get discouraged if they try to do too much at once. Your self-care goals should be realistic, not a set of New Year's resolutions that you'll discard when overwhelmed with a sense of futility. So, try this:

Write in your journal one thing you want to start or do more regularly. Break your goal into the smallest pieces possible. If you want to take more time for pleasure or fun, for example, what is one thing you can do for just a few minutes that you enjoy?

Now, anticipate obstacles and what you can do to overcome them. A good tool for this is "WOOP." WOOP stands for Wish, Outcome, Obstacle, Plan (Oettingen 2015). Write down in your journal what you want to do, what obstacles might complicate your efforts, and how you can overcome those obstacles.

Strive to take better care of yourself in this one way and, when you feel ready, add another goal, if you wish. Of course, you could transform many other wishes into plans at once, but be careful. Efforts at self-care should help you, not add to your stress.

Six weeks after she first saw Dr. Pérez for therapy, Anita's son Justin again didn't come home from school when he was supposed to. Anita felt the same panic surge through her. She had trouble breathing and began feeling lightheaded. For a few minutes, she sat on the sofa and focused on taking big, deep breaths. As she did so, her body started to calm down.

Her mind didn't calm down, however. She was imagining all the possible places Justin could be: in a ditch, on the side of a road, locked away in a bathroom doing who knows what. She pushed herself to also consider the benign possibilities. Maybe Justin had forgotten to tell her about a football practice. Or maybe he was chatting with a girl he liked at school and didn't want to be pulled away by his mother's annoying texts. Thinking of these possibilities helped Anita not to fall down a rabbit hole.

She still worried, of course. She reminded herself, This is a moment of suffering, *and she let herself feel the worry without judging herself. Then she went through other pieces of the self-compassion break, reminding herself not to push her feelings away, to accept them, and to respond with tenderness. With her hand on her shoulder, she told herself,* This is hard, but you're not alone. You can get through this.

Anita's husband was out of contact, so she called Imani. Her friend offered to come over, but Anita said she just wanted to talk on the phone. As she vented to Imani, Anita recognized that her pain was based on reality, not her mind's tendency to leap to the worst-case scenarios. Justin might be in danger. What should she do? She and Imani agreed she'd call the police if Justin didn't come home in a half hour.

Justin walked through the front door just a few minutes later. A teacher had held him after class to talk about submitting his English paper for a contest. The two got into such a rich conversation that Justin lost track of time. Anita yelled at him, "You're so self-absorbed! You nearly gave me a heart attack. Why are you so inconsiderate?" Justin said, "Sorry," shook his head, and went upstairs to his bedroom.

Tidal waves of emotion slammed Anita: anger, sadness, fear, regret. She was careful to take in deep breaths. Every time she had a negative thought about herself, she silently repeated it back to herself. "I shouldn't have gotten angry at Justin" became "I'm having the thought that I shouldn't have gotten angry at Justin." Her thought "Justin hates me right now" changed to "I'm having the thought that Justin hates me right now."

Anita recognized the cognitive distortions at work (should statements, labeling, catastrophizing, mind-reading, emotional reasoning). Looking at the evidence, she told herself, It's natural to get angry when you're scared. You'll apologize to him for losing your temper, and you'll work on managing your anger better. Even if you overreact sometimes, it's not always true. And you have no idea what he's thinking or feeling right now.

Taking deep breaths as she walked, Anita went upstairs, knocked on Justin's door, asked if she could come in and talk, and he opened the door.

You can use this chapter's self-help strategies to deal with the emotional and physical stress around your loved one's suicidality. The next chapter goes over ways to tackle the stress of asking someone if they have suicidal thoughts and not knowing what to say if the answer is yes.

CHAPTER 4

Asking Difficult Questions

Suicide remains unspeakable in many quarters—except, ironically, when people aren't truly talking about suicide. How often have you said something like, "This heat makes me want to die"? Or, "I'll kill myself if I have to sit through another long meeting"? Along the same lines, people casually speak of "political suicide," "suicide sprints," "suicide ski runs," and so on. But when it comes to truly talking about suicide, a strong taboo demands silence.

The taboo goes in both directions. People who think of suicide often are terrified of telling anyone, and others are terrified to ask. This chapter and the next go into different ways to talk with your loved one about their suicidal thoughts. Even if you already know your loved one is considering suicide, even if you've already talked about it with them, these conversations are seldom a one-time event. This information is relevant for future conversations.

Let's start with the example of Granger and Tabitha:

Nearly every day, Granger dreaded getting out of bed. At thirty-five, he hadn't kicked his addiction to alcohol, despite going through rehab twice. Granger believed he'd feel better about himself if only he could stop drinking, but he also didn't think he could stop drinking until he felt better about himself. Talk about a vicious cycle. Granger felt weak, flawed, and broken.

On a particularly bad morning, flattened under the covers, he kept thinking, You're a worthless piece of crap. You should kill yourself. *He called his girlfriend, Tabitha, at her job. After a few minutes of small talk, he told her he was having a bad morning. He mumbled into the phone, "Nothing's worth it anymore. I feel like giving up."*

Fear shot through Tabitha. That sounded ominous. Could he be thinking of killing himself? She didn't know how to ask. He might get angry or offended. Besides, if he were thinking about suicide, he would tell her, wouldn't he? She chided herself for overreacting.

"Thanks a lot," she said. "So, I'm not worth it anymore?"

Granger huffed a big sigh. "No, no, that's not what I meant. I just don't see things getting any better for me."

"Honey," she said, "things will get better. You just need to get up and get moving."

"Yeah, I guess you're right," Granger said. "I know I'll be fine." He felt a little guilty lying, but he suspected nobody could handle the truth.

Hidden Suicidal Thoughts

Imagine you're considering suicide. If you've ever been there, you might look back on that time or envision it happening now. If not, just pretend that one day, when you felt profoundly stressed or sad, this thought kept looping through your head: "I should kill myself." In your imaginary scenario, consider the following:

- Would you tell someone right away about your suicidal thoughts? Why or why not?

- What would you fear happening if people knew?

- What else would make it hard for you to tell others?

If, when considering this hypothetical, you think you'd have difficulty telling others about suicidal thoughts, you're not alone. Most people who think of suicide hide it to at least some degree (Hom et al. 2017). A lot of people hide their suicide attempts, too. A study of adolescents who survived an attempt revealed that one-third never told anybody, not even a parent (Levi-Belz et al. 2019). In cases where adolescents are considering suicide, many parents—roughly half, according to one study—have no idea (Jones et al. 2019).

People have various reasons for hiding their suicidal thoughts, based on my professional experiences and on published research. Common reasons for staying mum include:

I'm embarrassed.

Others will think I'm "crazy."

Someone will call the police.

The person I tell will take it personally.

I'll be committed to a mental hospital.

Nobody will believe me. They'll think I just want attention.

The person I tell won't care.

People will treat me differently.

I don't want people to watch me like a hawk.

I'll be rejected or judged.

I need to handle my problems on my own.

People will get angry at me.

Whoever I tell will change the subject, make a joke, or do something else dismissive.

The person I tell will freak out.

Nobody can help me.

I want to preserve my privacy.

People will think I'm weak or stupid.

They'll tell other people.

I hate for people to worry about me.

I don't want to be stopped.

Many people with hidden suicidal thoughts drop hints, consciously or not. They may tell jokes involving suicide, use euphemisms, or give cryptic clues. The celebrity chef Anthony Bourdain offers a striking example. In the years before he ultimately killed himself, he made numerous offhand remarks that if something bad happened to him, even something as minor as getting a bad cheeseburger at an airport, he'd kill himself. Ultimately, he died by suicide using the same method, and in the same type of establishment, he'd mentioned in a seemingly offhand remark. In another example, an emergency room physician, Loice Swisher, would quip, when colleagues at the hospital asked how things were going, "There is nothing going on here that a hundred units of insulin wouldn't cure" (Swisher 2016, 10). She said it so casually that people assumed she had a dark sense of humor. She was dead serious.

People can allude to suicidal thoughts in other ways, still without naming them. Like Granger in the example earlier, they might say life isn't worth living, or they want to give up. There are many other possibilities, too, such as:

I wish I'd never been born.

I'm thinking of doing something drastic.

Nobody will miss me when I'm gone.

I'm tired of living.

I can't take anymore.

I hate my life.

I don't have anything to contribute anymore.

It doesn't matter if I live or die.

There's nothing left for me.

I'd rather die.

What's the point of living?

If only I could go to sleep and never wake up.

I'm a burden to others.

I want to disappear.

Goodbye, world.

These expressions don't automatically mean a person is thinking of suicide. Many people have said things like, "I can't take it anymore," and, "I wish I'd never been born," without considering suicide. But those kinds of statements are worth asking about. "What do you mean when you say that you can't take it anymore?" or, "When you say you wish you'd never been born, do you mean you want to die?" are examples of direct questions you can ask.

What Frightens You About Asking?

If asking someone, "Are you thinking of suicide?" makes you nervous or afraid, you're in good company. The psychologist Paul Quinnett states that, even for psychotherapists, asking someone about suicidal thoughts "is one of the world's most unpleasant topics" (2019, 357). This fear helps explain the taboo and silence that stifle conversations about suicide.

Read over the following list and write down in your journal which of the following possibilities frightens you when it comes to asking someone about suicidal thoughts:

Talking about suicide will give the person the idea.

The person will get angry.

I won't know how to respond if the person says yes.

I'll get too emotional.

It's too intrusive to ask.

I won't be able to help.

I'm afraid of the answer.

It will make the person feel worse.

The person won't answer honestly.

I'll feel hurt or angry if the answer is yes.

I don't want the person to think I think they're crazy.

I'll say something that causes the person to act on suicidal thoughts.

I'm afraid of something else. (Write about this, too, in your journal.)

As you may have noticed while going over the list, fears around discussing suicide generally fall into three categories: fear of putting the idea of suicide in the person's head, fear of saying something wrong, and fear of feeling distressed yourself.

Fear of Planting the Idea

This fear paralyzes many people. Fortunately, it's the easiest to quiet, because it's just not true. Almost a dozen research studies consistently have shown that asking about suicidal thoughts doesn't give someone a new idea or cause a suicide attempt (Polihronis et al. 2020). Even if the person you're worried about is an adolescent, they've almost certainly known about suicide for many years. Most children understand by first grade that some people end their own lives, though they usually don't know the word "suicide" yet (Mishara 1999). Beyond that, suicide comes up frequently in the news, social media, books, movies, songs, memes, and video games.

Fear of Saying Something Wrong

Most people don't get stressed or upset if they're asked about suicide, but a small percentage do (Blades et al. 2018). Those feelings pass, and there's no evidence the momentary distress increases danger.

That leads to another fear: *What if I say something that makes the person act on their suicidal thoughts?* What a tormenting thought. The reality is, unless you actually encourage someone to act on their suicidal thoughts, your words are unlikely to be dangerous.

You also might fear angering someone. Suicide is so taboo that asking about it can feel like an invasion of privacy. Yet, people tend to understand. I've asked hundreds—maybe thousands—of people if they have suicidal thoughts. Most people I ask say matter-of-factly yes or no, and we go from there. Some emphatically say no, they're not thinking of suicide, and they explain why. And then there are the people who bow their head, or cry, or hesitate, and whisper, "Yes." They've never told anybody before, and unburdening their secret brings relief.

It's understandable if you fear saying something that upsets or angers the person, and I hope this fear won't silence you. Yes, some things are better to say than others, as you'll see in the next chapter. But you're human, and nobody's perfect. Be compassionate with yourself and remember you can clarify, correct, and apologize if your well-intentioned questions upset the person.

Fear of Feeling Distressed

It's upsetting to learn someone you love is thinking of suicide. Maybe you're scared of the answer. Or maybe you're scared learning of someone's suicidal thoughts will have some kind of contagion effect and your own mental state will deteriorate. These are understandable fears. It can be quite distressing to hear about your loved one's suicidal thoughts. That's why it's important to practice good self-care, seek support when needed, and use stress management techniques covered in chapter 3. Isn't it better to bear some emotional discomfort now, in the service of helping your loved one, than to later regret avoiding the topic?

You also might fear feeling helpless. So many variables are beyond your control. This is painful to accept, but some feelings of helplessness are inescapable. Even among highly trained mental health professionals, no method is guaranteed to uncover someone's suicidal thoughts, predict who will attempt suicide, or prevent suicide. You might not be able to get rid of all your helpless feelings, but you can reduce them. Knowledge really is power. By reading this book, you're learning how to converse about suicidal thoughts in ways that can support someone to speak their truth.

Managing Your Fears

Fear isn't necessarily bad. Often, being afraid motivates you to do something better. When it comes to asking about suicidal thoughts, healthy fear can prompt you to ask questions directly, listen attentively and empathetically, and in general, help the person the best you can.

Fear becomes a problem when it hurts your ability to help. If you're too afraid, you might never ask about suicide. And if someone does disclose suicidal thoughts, your fear might thwart you from listening fully. Fear can also lead you to unnecessarily call the police, react with anger, or become so distraught that the person is reluctant to talk with you about their problems. These possibilities make it all the more important that you understand—and resolve, the best you can—what frightens you.

Information helps weaken fear, but the head and heart often don't communicate with each other: You can know logically that it's safe to talk about suicide, for example, while your heart insists it's not. Fear sometimes has a louder voice. You can talk back to it.

The following questions, adapted from the psychologist Judith Beck (2021), might help you tame your fears. Write your responses in your journal:

- What scares you the most about asking someone you love about suicidal thoughts?

- What's the worst that could happen if you ask?

- How likely do you think it is that the worst will happen, on a scale of 0 percent to 100 percent?

- What's the worst that could happen if you do *not* ask the person you love about possible suicidal thoughts?

- What's the best that could happen if you initiate the conversation?

- What do you think will probably happen if you ask?

- What would you say to someone who's afraid to ask another person about suicidal thoughts?

- What can you tell yourself to soothe your fears?

Whatever frightens you, which is worse: to ask someone about suicidal thoughts despite your fears, or to not ask and possibly remain unaware the person is thinking of suicide? If you don't ask, you won't know, and you could miss a chance to help.

I don't mean to minimize or pooh-pooh your misgivings. Feeling afraid is often unavoidable. Keep in mind a popular self-help phrase: Feel the fear and do it anyway (Jeffers 1987). Your loved one's life is at stake. The good news is you can learn ways to ask about suicide that might lessen your anxiety and the other person's discomfort.

Asking About Suicidal Thoughts

The shame, stigma, and fears around suicide make it all the more important that you broach the topic sensitively and listen nonjudgmentally. This section contains information that can make future conversations on the topic more fruitful for both you and your loved one.

Building Up

One way to ask about suicidal thoughts is to build up to the question. You can start by saying you've noticed the person's under a lot of stress or struggling in some other way and asking what's going on. With each question, you get progressively closer to asking about suicidal thoughts. In this conversation between Jasper, twenty-four, and his older sister Heidi, you can see this incremental approach:

Jasper: "You've seemed upset lately, Heidi, like maybe you're under a lot of stress."

Heidi: "Actually, yes, I'm having a really hard time."

Jasper: "What's going on?"

Heidi: "I feel trapped. I hate being a lawyer, but there's nothing else I can do that would pay so well."

Jasper: "That really sucks. Do you ever feel so bad that you wish you were dead?"

Heidi: "Actually, yeah, the thought has crossed my mind. If I was dead, I wouldn't have to sit through another deposition ever again."

Jasper: "Do you think of killing yourself?"

Heidi: "That thought has crossed my mind, too."

Another approach is to invoke other people's experiences with suicidal thoughts. This shows you know it's common to consider suicide and you won't judge. For example, before asking Heidi if she ever wishes she were dead, Jasper could say, "A lot of people who hate their work feel so miserable that sometimes they wish they were dead. Do you?"

The psychiatrist Shawn Shea (1999) calls this "normalizing" suicidal thoughts. You're not conveying suicide itself is normal, only that thinking of suicide isn't shocking or "crazy." You can handle talking about it—and listening.

Naming Suicide

If you use coded language of some kind ("Are you thinking of doing something drastic?"), you risk sending the message that suicide is unspeakable and you're afraid to talk about it. Vague language like, "Are you thinking of harming yourself?" can lead to vague or incorrect answers. Some people who hurt themselves on purpose have no suicidal intent, and some people who attempt suicide view death as helping, not harming, themselves. Equally important, by clearly asking about suicidal thoughts, you show the person you're not afraid to talk about it. Here are examples of direct language:

"Do you have suicidal thoughts?"

"Are you thinking of killing yourself?"

"Do you want to end your life?"

Some people complain it's culturally insensitive within some groups to ask so directly about suicide. You'll need to gauge whether, in your situation, the risk of cultural insensitivity outweighs the risk of not asking. It's possible the person is scared to tell you they're thinking of suicide precisely because the topic is off-limits, and your asking the question would show you welcome the conversation.

Avoiding Leading Questions

As much as you might hope the person isn't considering suicide, be careful not to steer them to the answer you want to hear. For example, some people ask, "You're not thinking of suicide, are you?" This wording reveals your bias. If you doubt me, imagine someone asks you, "You're not going to eat the last chocolate chip cookie, are you?" As another example, some people ask, "Are you thinking of doing something stupid?" This shows how you want the person to answer. After all, who wants to admit to stupidity?

If the Answer Is No

In case the person is withholding the truth, I recommend not heaving a huge sigh of relief and dropping the topic. Remember, they might be too scared or anxious to tell the truth. Imagine you exclaim, "Oh, good. I was worried. I'm so happy you're not thinking of suicide." The person might feel grateful you don't know.

One way to continue the conversation is to ask, "If you have suicidal thoughts in the future, would you feel okay telling me?" When I ask my psychotherapy clients this question, people often say, "No, absolutely not." I ask why, and almost every time, they tell me they're scared that I'll have them hospitalized if they're thinking of suicide. I clarify that suicidal thoughts, by themselves, aren't a reason for hospitalization and that I generally recommend hospitalization only in extreme cases, like when someone is resolved to end their life today, no matter what. After I say that, many clients say something along the lines of, "Oh, I'm not thinking of suicide that seriously. I only think of it when I'm super stressed, and I don't think I'd really do it." Now we're having a conversation about thoughts that, only minutes earlier, the person denied having.

The same thing might happen to you. Your loved one might say they wouldn't tell you about suicidal thoughts because you'd call the police. You could explain you'd call the police only if they had a weapon in hand—or whatever your threshold might be. Or your loved one might say, "If I had suicidal thoughts, I wouldn't want to dump that on you." And you can make clear you'd much rather know than not know, no matter what.

If the Person Doesn't Answer

If you're a parent and you're concerned about your adolescent, don't be surprised if they say sarcastically something along the lines of, "Yeah, right, like I'd ever tell you." Adults, too, may shy away from the topic, make a joke, or do something else to avoid answering. How frustrating!

Ultimately, you can't force someone to tell you what they're thinking. Pressuring the person for a response can push them further into silence.

For teens and adults who refuse your direct questions, make clear you'd like to know because you care and you hope in the future the person will feel comfortable telling you. You could also try to discuss what makes the conversation hard. This puts the focus on the process, rather than the content, of talking about a difficult topic.

> When Yoshiro, thirty-one, asked his older sister Hiroko if she had suicidal thoughts, Hiroko shook her head and said, "I'm not going to tell you that."
>
> "I know it's up to you to tell me or not," Yoshiro said. "But could you maybe say why you don't want to? Maybe there's something I could do to make it easier."
>
> "I'm not saying I have suicidal thoughts, but if I did, I wouldn't tell you because you'd think I was mental," Hiroko said.
>
> "I don't think people with suicidal thoughts are 'crazy,'" Yoshiro told his sister. "They're trying to solve a problem."

Hiroko changed the subject, but a couple days later, when her suicidal thoughts intensified, she called her brother and confided in him.

If your loved one evades the question and you have reasons to believe the person is considering suicide, consider proceeding as if the answer were yes. You'll read in chapters 6 and 7 about possible steps to take. For now, let's return to the conversation between Granger and Tabitha from earlier in the chapter.

Tabitha couldn't stop worrying about Granger. She called him back and said, "Honey, when you said, 'Nothing's worth it anymore,' it made me wonder what you meant."

He sighed loudly. "I just don't know if it's worth it to get out of bed."

It felt like someone was stepping on Tabitha's stomach—that's how afraid she was to ask Granger if he had suicidal thoughts. She took an extra deep breath and resolved to push through her fear.

"A lot of people, when they feel it's not worth it to get out of bed, they're thinking of dying," she said. "Are you thinking of suicide?"

"No way," Granger said. "I just don't want to get out of bed."

Tabitha wanted to jump with joy upon hearing his "No way." She kept her relief to herself, in case he wasn't telling her the whole story.

"It makes me wonder," Tabitha asked, "if you ever did have suicidal thoughts, would you tell me?"

Granger laughed for the first time that day. "Um, I don't think so," he said. "That's a big N-O."

"Why, though?" Tabitha asked.

"You'd freak out. And you'd call the police."

"Honey, I wouldn't call the police unless, like, you had a gun to your head," she said. "I swear, if you had suicidal thoughts, I'd want to talk with you about it and help you. I don't think I'd freak out. I'm not freaking out now, am I? And I just asked you if you're thinking of suicide."

"But I said no," Granger said, "so you don't have a reason to freak out."

"Right, but I was worried you'd say yes, and I didn't freak out. I could have handled it if you did."

"Be honest," he said, "wouldn't you have called 911 if I'd said yes?"

"No, I really wouldn't, not unless you were going to kill yourself right now," Tabitha said.

"Promise?"

"Yes, I promise."

"Okay," he said, "I might as well tell you. I have been lying here in bed wondering if I should just off myself."

Tabitha's stomach fluttered with fear again. She knew her reaction could make the difference between Granger confiding in her more, or closing the door on the conversation and locking her out.

Once you've established that someone is thinking of suicide, your task is to learn more. Unless you believe the person is in immediate danger and needs emergency assistance, first listen, ask questions, and make statements that invite the person to say more. The next chapter goes over these steps, and then we'll continue the conversation between Tabitha and Granger.

CHAPTER 5

Brave Listening

If someone tells you that, yes, they're considering suicide, they might retreat if you're judgmental, overly upset, angry, or closed off in some other way to hearing about it. At a minimum, the person might conceal the true extent of their suicidal thoughts. At the most extreme, they might take it back altogether: "I was just joking" or "I didn't mean it. I just wanted to see what you'd say." You're more likely to keep the conversation going if you respond with empathy and compassion, withhold judgment, refrain from immediately trying to persuade the person not to think of suicide, and demonstrate you're listening and trying to understand.

Experts in communication refer to these acts as "active listening," "reflective listening," and "empathic listening." For our purposes, I prefer the term "brave listening." It takes courage to ask questions whose answers you fear. So does listening to what hurts to hear.

Brave listening is resisting the temptation to change the subject, give advice, lecture, offer reassurance, or convince the person to think or feel differently. It's focusing on the person's needs, not on your own wish to feel less helpless, worried, and stressed as you listen.

Some people don't listen at all, bravely or otherwise, when someone confides suicidal thoughts. They call the police, rush the person to an emergency room, hand out the number for the suicide hotline, or advise the person to talk with a therapist. Or they immediately launch into reassurance, affirmations, and advice in a campaign to change the person's mind. These all can be valid options, depending on the context. But if you instantly jump into emergency or fix-it mode, your loved one might feel rejected and misunderstood.

In this chapter, I go over the principles of listening well. I also alert you to responses that often are counterproductive and what you can say instead. First, a couple caveats: The guidance in this book is no guarantee. Even if you say everything "right," even if you listen bravely and nonjudgmentally, even if you connect the person with professional help and help the person stick to their safety plan—in short, even if you do everything you can—the person still might end their life. You can only do your best; you can't do everything. Which leads me to a second caveat:

If you've already experienced the suicide of someone you love, the guidance in this chapter could stir up pain and self-doubt. What you said or did then might have gone against the advice you'll read here. Let me be clear: The actions you took or did not take don't mean the suicide was your fault. This book describes some ideal ways to respond, but the reality is most people never have learned them. Even among mental health professionals, few have received much training on how to help someone with suicidal thoughts (Labouliere et al. 2021). So, please have compassion for yourself if you learn something now that makes you regret something you said then.

What Would You Say?

Imagine your loved one says to you, "I'm a bad person and I don't deserve to live." They're being sincere. And, to you, preposterous. You have no doubt they're a good person and in no way deserve to die. Reading the following list of possible responses, make a mental note of which ones you might say.

- "Don't say that about yourself. It hurts to hear you talk that way."

- "That's not true. You absolutely deserve to live."

- "You're a good person! Think of all the good things you've done and all your good qualities, such as..."

- "How could you possibly think that? You're not being rational."

- "Whatever mistakes you've made, you haven't done anything that bad."

- "Things can't be as bad as they seem to you right now. You'll feel better soon."

- "You really feel bad about yourself right now."

- "Those kinds of feelings are so painful."

- "It seems like you wish you were a better person in some way."

- "What's happened to make you feel you deserve to die?"

- "You're really going through a difficult time, aren't you?"

- "I don't agree, but I'd like to understand why you believe you're a bad person and don't deserve to live. Can you tell me more?"

If the last six responses matched how you'd respond more than the first six, you already have solid instincts for listening bravely. In contrast, many people are inclined to react to the statement, "I'm a bad person and I don't deserve to live," with some kind of reassurance, dissuasion, or disbelief. Often, those well-intentioned efforts to cheer someone up can discourage the person from sharing more. There's a time and place to help the person challenge their thinking, which chapter 11 discusses. If premature, however, those efforts can short-circuit the conversation.

It's not easy to listen to people express self-hatred, hopelessness, and suicidal thoughts. Fear can stand in the way of your really hearing what the person is saying. In the previous chapter, you looked at your fears of asking about suicidal thoughts. Now, imagine the person's said yes, they're thinking of suicide. Would any of the following fears deter you from listening bravely?

- If I don't try to help my loved one feel better right away, they will feel worse.

- I'm scared I'll get sad or depressed if the person talks about how bad things are.

- I'll feel unbearably helpless if I "just" listen and don't try to fix things.

- The person will never stop talking, and I can't take hours to hear their life story.

- If I let someone wallow in negativity, I'll be encouraging a "pity party."

- I'll seem incompetent or ineffective if I don't get the person's mind off their problems.

- I don't want to get dragged down by their drama.

- If I don't try to steer the conversation in a different direction, I'll be reminded of my own suicidal thoughts or the suicide of someone I know, and I won't be able to cope.

- The person will think I agree with their negative view if I don't rebut what they say.

- Unless I keep things light, I'll sound unnatural, like I'm trying to "therapize" the person.

It's not surprising if any of the fears above resonated with you. You have your own worries, needs, and stress, not to mention habits of listening that you've solidified over the years. These realities can make it hard to truly stay present. Still, no matter how old you are, it's possible to learn ways to listen better.

Listening bravely doesn't require a degree or letters behind your name, only a desire to understand and help. Customer service employees often receive training in active listening skills from their employer. Parents learn these skills in parenting classes and books such as *How to Talk So Kids Will Listen & Listen So Kids Will Talk* (Faber and Mazlish 2012).

Brave listening isn't complex. It can mean saying, "That's so stressful," instead of, "I'm sure it will all work out," when you can't know it will all work out. Brave listening can mean encouraging the person to keep talking by just nodding your head or making small statements, like "Uh-huh," "You're feeling really stressed," and "Tell me more." These responses incorporate key ingredients of listening: empathy, validation, and reflection.

Empathy

To empathize is to understand the situation from someone else's point of view, even when you disagree. Consider this conversation between Lizbeth and her seventeen-year-old son, Daniel.

When Lizbeth got home from the store, Daniel was pacing back and forth in the living room. "I screwed up at work," he told her. "I really screwed up."

Lizbeth's shoulders tensed. She waited to hear what disaster had occurred.

"I'm so stupid," Daniel said. "I told my boss 'goodbye' when I left after my shift ended. I should've said 'see you tomorrow.' Goodbye is so final. He might think I'm never coming back."

Lizbeth felt tempted to laugh. Daniel was hyper-analyzing a word that his boss at the pizza place probably didn't even notice, let alone fret about. But she knew that, to her worried son, it was anything but absurd. Her judgment wasn't likely to instantly change his mind. So, instead of trying to talk him out of his feelings, she acknowledged them.

"You're really worried," she said, and Daniel nodded, still pacing.

"Are you worried he'll read something bad into your saying goodbye, and you don't want to jeopardize your job or upset him?" Lizbeth asked.

"Exactly," he said. "I'm scared he thinks I quit.'"

"I know how much this job means to you," Lizbeth said.

"Right, I need the money for prom," Daniel said. "But maybe he didn't really think I quit. What do you think?"

"Well, since you asked, I think it's possible it didn't even occur to him. People say goodbye all the time without it meaning forever."

"True," Daniel said, and, for the first time in a half hour, he stopped pacing.

If Lizbeth had replied without empathy—"Don't be ridiculous," for example, or, "It's not as big of a deal as you think," or, "You're overreacting"— then Daniel most likely would've felt unwelcome to share more. They might have argued, or he might have silently sulked off to his bedroom and shut the door. Lizbeth's empathetic response helped him to recognize from within that there was a different way of looking at things.

There's no one right way to respond, by the way. In this case, Lizbeth could've said, "Tell me what happened," or, "That's so stressful for you," or just given him a hug, or done something else to help him feel connected, seen, and understood. These are also validating responses.

Validation

In the context of listening, validation doesn't mean you agree with what the person says. Rather, it involves conveying that the person's feelings are understandable from their vantage point. In contrast, an invalidating response would be to suggest the person is overreacting, neurotic, silly, or outright wrong for feeling what they feel. "Stop crying," "You shouldn't be upset," "Don't be ridiculous / get hysterical / worry so much," "Calm down," and "Man up" are examples of invalidating responses that are all too common.

You can always find something to validate. In the example above, Lizbeth wasn't agreeing with Daniel that his utterance of the word "goodbye" was catastrophic. She validated that he felt anxious because he wants to keep his job.

If someone discloses suicidal thoughts to you, you can validate their feelings by acknowledging how they're feeling, without judgment. Some examples:

"Things must be really rough right now if you're thinking of suicide."

"You're really struggling, aren't you?"

"A lot of people think of suicide when they don't see any other way out of their problems."

"We're wired to escape pain, so it makes sense you'd think of suicide if you believe you'll never stop hurting."

Do you feel anxious when you think of saying those things—sort of like you're agreeing with the person that they should consider suicide? If so, you can follow up with something like, "I'm not saying you should kill yourself, believe me!" or, "I personally think things will get better for you, but I can see that you feel pretty hopeless." You're still showing you can see it from the person's perspective, their feelings are understandable, and you're inviting them to say more.

Reflection

You can reflect what someone's said by paraphrasing, summarizing key statements, or simply repeating back a few words. This prompts the person to keep going, not so much because of what you've said but because of what you have *not* said. You haven't disagreed, changed the subject, given advice, minimized the person's concerns, judged, launched into your own experiences, professed to understand when you don't, or tried to change the person's mind. By reflecting what you hear, you allow someone to feel heard and understood—and, importantly, to correct you if you've misunderstood.

When reflecting, avoid formulaically parroting what the person said. Repeat words when it feels appropriate, but strive more often to restate the essence, which can relate to feelings or content. Using the example of someone who believes they're bad and doesn't deserve to live, a reflection of content could be, "You think you deserve to die." You can reflect emotion by saying, "You feel really bad about yourself."

You can try listening bravely right now. It doesn't always require a whole conversation to listen well—you can demonstrate understanding with a single line. But for this exercise, have a conversation with your loved one about how they're feeling. You might want to let the person know you're going to try out tips from this book, in case they notice you're acting differently. Practice listening bravely by doing the following:

- Ask about something stressful that the person's been facing.

- As the person talks, resist offering advice, sharing your own experiences, or trying to cheer the person up, at least at first.

- Repeat back the content or emotion of what the person says. You might start with, "It sounds like you…" or, "I hear you saying you…" or, "From what you said, you…"

- Check your understanding. After briefly summarizing what you've heard, you could ask, "Do I have that right?" or, "Have I understood correctly?"

- Ask open-ended questions to learn more. As the person speaks, use "minimal encouragers," short statements or sounds that show you're listening and want to hear more. Examples include "Mmm-hmm," "Uh-huh," "I see," and gestures like smiling or nodding your head.

- Continue to follow these steps until the exploration reaches a natural turning point, if possible. Often, the other person naturally moves into problem-solving on their own or asks for your advice. Or they might just change the subject or say something like, "Thanks for listening."

After you try out brave listening, answer the following questions in your journal, both to gain clarity now and, someday, to see what progress you've made.

- How did it feel to do this exercise with your loved one? That is, did it feel difficult, awkward, fake, silly, or different in some other way to purely listen and reflect?

- What were you tempted to say, but didn't?

- What else, if anything, made it hard to stick with listening and reflecting?

- What did you learn that might have remained unsaid if you'd responded in your usual way?

- Would you want to be listened to this way? Why or why not?

Brave listening doesn't come naturally. It can feel stilted and uncomfortable, especially at first. Be patient. You wouldn't expect to speak a foreign language after just a few lessons. You'd need to practice many times to become fluent, and even then it's inevitable you'd make mistakes. The same is true with trying to listen differently. It takes practice.

What Not to Say

In contrast to brave listening, let's discuss counterproductive ways to respond when your loved one discloses suicidal thoughts. What works for you and the person you love might be different, but I want to alert you to common pitfalls.

Don't Deny or Dismiss

If someone tells you they're thinking of suicide, avoid making statements that minimize, dismiss, or deny the person's experience. Here are some examples:

"You don't really mean that."

"Don't be silly. You have so much to live for."

"But you're so young/ accomplished/ loved/ supported/ full of potential. You don't realize how good you have it."

"What do you have to feel suicidal about? You don't even have real problems." (This last one is often said to teens.)

Maybe you really are doubtful that the person has suicidal thoughts. You might suspect they're being manipulative or, as I hear often, "They just want attention." Recognize your stance is a belief, not necessarily a fact. What if you're wrong? It's better to believe someone who turns out not to be suicidal than to disbelieve someone who is. And if someone is pretending, there's usually something else going on that they do need help for.

Doubt, often, is actually denial. Denial is a powerful defense mechanism against sadness, anger, fear, anxiety, and other distressing feelings. You might disbelieve your loved one because the truth is so hard to bear. This example of Ram and his thirteen-year-old daughter, Shanti, shows denial at work:

One Saturday afternoon, Ram went inside Shanti's bedroom to deliver clean laundry. As he put the laundry basket on her bed, he noticed something poking out from beneath a pillow. It was his pistol, which he usually kept far in the back of his desk drawer. Also under the pillow was a handwritten note, in which Shanti revealed she wanted to kill herself.

As Ram read the note, Shanti walked into her room. Shaking with anger, Ram yelled at her for taking his gun without his permission. But he didn't ask about the note or Shanti's suicidal thoughts. He didn't believe her.

"She knew I'd find the gun," Ram told his wife later that evening. "She never would've used it. She just wants to know we care." It was easier to doubt his daughter wanted to die than to grasp the enormity of her pain and danger.

Don't Panic

Despite what you might hear or read elsewhere, suicidal thoughts aren't always a crisis. If someone appears to be on the verge of attempting suicide or just made an attempt, it's almost certainly an emergency. If not, take a few deep breaths, remind yourself that this is a precious opportunity to help, and keep listening, reflecting, and encouraging the person to tell you more.

Don't Focus on Your Feelings

You may experience a torrent of emotion, understandably, when your teen, partner, friend, or other loved one talks about thoughts of ending their life. Anxiety, panic, sadness, anger, and bewilderment are quite common. If you focus on your feelings, your loved one might feel obligated to take care of you, by saying things like, "Don't worry, I won't kill myself. I promise. I'm sorry for scaring you." Meanwhile, the person might change the subject, to avoid upsetting you more.

Don't Persuade

You want your loved one to resist suicidal thoughts, recover, and live. Of course you do. You might, as a result, want to persuade the person of all the reasons why they're wrong for considering suicide. As chapter 9 explains in more depth, this stance can put you and the person on opposite sides of an argument. If you argue against suicide, the person might be inclined to argue for it. It's usually better to listen, reflect, and help the person get in touch with their own reasons for not dying by suicide.

Don't Try to Fix It

It's natural to want to help the person solve their problems, feel better, and have no reason to consider suicide. Natural, but not always helpful, particularly if it preempts your listening to the person. People often offer advice like:

"Have you tried yoga/ exercise/ therapy/ antidepressants?"

"Here's what you can do to fix your situation."

"You need to not take things so seriously."

"Everything will work out fine. You'll see."

Superficial, pat, or unworkable suggestions can alienate people. Your loved one might think you just don't get it. Try to get it. Problem-solving, reassurance, and affirmations can be helpful in the right context. They're premature when used to avoid staying present with someone in their distress.

Don't Lecture or Judge

If you're religious and believe suicide is a violation of God's commandment "Thou shall not kill," now's not the time to share those beliefs. Reacting with judgment can compound feelings of shame and fear and cause the person to shut down.

Other examples of judgmental responses that can derail the conversation:

"Suicide is selfish/cowardly/weak/wrong."

"You're too sensitive."

"I went through far worse than you, and I never wanted to kill myself."

"You need to think more positively."

"Don't be such a drama queen."

Good motivations might underlie a judgmental response: you hope it will motivate your loved one to reject suicide. That's understandable, but judgments and lectures rarely get someone to change their suicidal thoughts. Even if the person says, "Yes, you're right," they might be saying it only to avoid your disapproval. Remember, suicidal thoughts can persist whether someone wants them to or not. Your negative judgments could scare someone away from confiding in you again.

Don't Say, "I Understand What You're Going Through" If You Don't

If you tell the person you understand, you almost certainly mean well, but do you truly understand what they're experiencing? If the person doesn't truly feel understood, your assertion could make them think you can't possibly understand.

Consider the example of Sgt. Kevin Briggs, a California highway patrol officer who successfully talked two hundred people out of jumping off the Golden Gate Bridge. After the individuals made the decision not to jump, Sgt. Briggs would ask them what he said that helped—and what didn't help. "Things that did not go well were, 'I understand.' That makes people angry," Briggs says. "Because you don't understand, and I totally get that now. I do not understand what is going on with that person. That is a very poor thing to say" (Hay 2015).

Don't "Guilt" the Person

This one is a little tricky. A great many people resist acting on their suicidal thoughts precisely because they don't want to hurt the people they love. *It would kill my partner. I couldn't do that to my children. My mother would never get over it.* A popular saying is, "Suicide doesn't end the pain. It just passes it on to others." So, should you point out to someone with suicidal thoughts how much their suicide would hurt others?

On the one hand, r/SuicideWatch, a peer-support group on Reddit .com for people with suicidal thoughts, forbids any posts that include "any guilt-tripping like 'Suicide is selfish' or 'Think of your loved ones,'" according to the site's guidelines. Those kinds of messages are considered to be abusive. On the other hand, many people have been dissuaded from suicide by these arguments. Take, for example, this true story:

> *Kevin Berthia was twenty-two years old when he hopped over the railing of the Golden Gate Bridge, intending to jump into the bay below. Kevin Briggs, the California highway patrol sergeant mentioned earlier, rushed to talk with him. For the next ninety-two minutes, standing on a pipe that ran just below the bridge and holding on to the bridge railing with his head bowed, Kevin told the officer why he wanted to die. Sgt. Briggs urged the young man to stay alive for his daughter, not yet one year old. "He reminded me that, Kevin, you need to be here for her next birthday... I was looking for a reason to live, and he gave me one" (Hope Inc. Stories 2021).*

It worked for Kevin Berthia—a stranger beseeched him to stay alive for his daughter, and he decided not to jump. So, asking someone to live for the sake of others could work, but it also can backfire.

Pressuring someone to stay alive for other people's sake can deter the person from saying more, especially if you haven't truly listened to the person. You risk conveying that you care more about your and others' potential pain in the future than your loved one's actual pain right now. On top of that, the person also might already feel guilty for thinking of suicide, knowing how much it would hurt others. They might feel judged by you, even shamed.

There's another factor to consider, too: people's motives for suicide are complex and unpredictable. It's not uncommon for someone to hope their death will trigger others' remorse. For example, someone might say, "If I kill myself, my parents will realize they should have treated me better." There's also a possibility, mercifully quite small, that the person is considering killing other people, too, to spare them the aftermath of suicide loss. It's painful to think about, but this is one of the main reasons why some mothers who die by suicide first kill their children (Sidebotham 2017).

The possibility of "guilting" or shaming someone for their suicidal thoughts doesn't mean you should avoid talking about your feelings. It depends on how you do it. There's a difference between saying, "Don't you know how much it'd hurt me if you killed yourself? How could you think of doing that to me?" and, "I love you and would be so sad if you died. I want to help you feel better so you'll stay." One response puts the focus on you and your needs. The other focuses on the other person's needs, too. And, with the latter option, you're not implying the person should stop thinking of suicide for your sake.

It's also fair for you to point out where a person's not thinking logically. If someone says, "Nobody will miss me when I'm gone," listen, reflect, and explore—at first. For example, you could say, "You really feel nobody would care if you died. What's happened to make you feel that way?" Once you've listened, saying you're certain such-and-such people would miss the person is a statement of fact, not a ploy to whip up guilt. Pointing out these inconsistencies is fine, as long as you don't focus on logic over emotion as a way to avoid listening bravely.

One other thing: While I don't recommend guilting someone about suicide, do dive into their feelings of guilt if the person brings it up. That way, you're following their lead and, hopefully, helping the person get more in touch with their own motivation to stay alive. Here's an example:

> Steven, twenty-four, told his older brother Vincent, "The only thing that stops me from offing myself is Mom and Dad. I know nobody wants their kid to die."
>
> Vincent resisted the temptation to say, "Damn straight. Don't be an asshole." He wanted to keep the conversation going, so he reflected, "Mom and Dad are a big reason you won't kill yourself."
>
> "Yeah, so far," Steven said. "Them, and I don't know, maybe you'd miss me, too."
>
> "You think?" Vincent said. He punched him lightly in the shoulder. "Doofus, you're my kid brother. I don't want anything bad to happen to you. What can I do to help?"

Don't Give an Ultimatum

Demanding someone stop thinking of suicide isn't likely to make the thoughts vanish. Instead, it might make the person less likely to confide in you again about their wish to die, lest they "violate" an ultimatum or promise. Likewise, countless people have attempted or died by suicide after promising not to do so. A better approach is to help your loved one think through how they can resist acting on suicidal thoughts. Chapter 7 explains this process.

Don't Dare the Person

Some people say things like, "If you were really serious about wanting to kill yourself, you'd kill yourself," or, "Go ahead and do it." I expect you know this already, but just in case: don't ever dare someone to act on their suicidal thoughts.

People who make these kinds of statements usually believe "reverse psychology" will make thoughts of suicide go away. Or they believe their loved one isn't really thinking of suicide and by pushing the person to act, the truth will come out. "I called his bluff," a father said of his teenage son. "I went to the garage, got my hunting knife, put it on the kitchen table in front of him, and told him, 'Here you go. If you really mean it, you'll need this.'"

It's not hard to imagine how rejected someone could feel if they worked up the nerve to talk about their suicidal thoughts and the other person said, in one way or another, "Just do it." Tragically, there are many documented cases of "suicide baiting," where people killed themselves after being cheered on or dared by others (Phillips and Mann 2019).

What to Say

Now that we've looked at responses to try to avoid, let's talk about what to try instead when someone talks about their suicidal thoughts. Please consider the following material to be suggestions, not a script or rigid instructions. This chapter lays out some ideal ways to communicate about suicidal thoughts, and reality often looks quite different. As in all of life, imperfection is inevitable. Try to relax. If you're too preoccupied with what to say next, you'll miss out on truly listening. In most cases, how you listen is more important than what you say.

Also, these suggestions might not work for everyone. Some people might appreciate hearing something that's not suggested here, and others might despise what is suggested. Everyone is different. Check in with your loved one to see how the conversation feels and ask how you could be more helpful.

Show Appreciation

Very often, people are frightened, nervous, or embarrassed to talk about their suicidal thoughts. Expressing gratitude to your loved one for telling you helps convey that you want to know, you're not judging, and you can handle this tough topic. Here are some examples:

"I'm grateful you told me, so I can try to help."

"Thank you for letting me know. You shouldn't have to deal with this alone."

"I'd always want to know if you have suicidal thoughts."

Learn More

As a friend, family member, or other loved one, you can't be expected to conduct a formal suicide risk assessment. Still, learning more about what the person's experiencing can help you better understand if emergency help is needed. Not incidentally, it can also help the person to feel connected, heard, and understood, which is no small thing.

You might be immediately tempted to barrage the person with questions: *Do you think you'll kill yourself? When? How? Have you already tried?* These are important questions to ask, but unless the person's in an urgent state of danger, like they've just overdosed or are holding a weapon, I recommend first inviting the person to tell you more on their own terms. Here are a few possibilities:

"You're feeling really bad if you're thinking of suicide. What's going on?"

"It sounds like you're really struggling. Do you feel comfortable telling me more?"

"What's making you think of suicide?"

After you've listened, the other questions are important, too. Learning the extent of the suicidal person's thinking can let you know what kind of help is needed. The more you learn about the person's planning and intent, the better. Here are some questions you might ask:

Have you made a plan to kill yourself?

What ways have you thought of killing yourself?

How much do you intend to act on your suicidal thoughts?

Have you already made a suicide attempt? (When, if so?)

Try not to ask these questions one after the other. Aim for a conversation, not an interrogation. At the same time, there's no one right way, and you might discover an approach that works better for you and your loved one.

Express Empathy and Compassion

Even though it's impossible to fully understand what a person's thinking and feeling, you can try. Acknowledge the person's struggles, as well as their emotions, without judgment. Some possible things to say:

"It seems like you don't see any other ways to end your pain."

"You're really hurting, aren't you?"

"It sounds like you're under a lot of stress."

Remember, as much as you might want to, you don't need to fix your loved one's problems or cheer them up. You can just be present. Never underestimate the power of comments that support, but don't fix:

"I had no idea things were so bad for you. I'm sorry it's been so hard."

"I'm grateful you're still here. I love you and don't want you to die."

"I want to help you get through this."

You also don't have to say anything at all. You can just sit with the person, be present, give a hug, or show you care in other ways.

Address (Not) Being a Burden

Your loved one might think your life would be easier if they died. "I'm dragging you down," Latisha told her husband. "You'll get over me after I'm gone, and you'll find someone who can make you happy."

Let's be frank here: You really might feel burdened in some way. You might be losing time, money, energy, sleep, and peace of mind while attending to your loved one's crises. It's not irrational for the person to see those changes as a burden for you. What is irrational is for the person to think their death would be easier to bear.

I'm not suggesting you tell the person, "Yes, you are a burden." Listen bravely. Learn why they worry they're bringing you down. Don't rebut immediately. Try to understand and empathize. That way, you'll have added credibility when you say that whatever problems your loved one's suicidal thoughts or other conditions pose, you'd far rather deal with those than the much larger, irrevocable burden of their death.

Convey Hope

After you've truly listened to the person, it's appropriate—and important—to try to generate some hope. You can borrow from tools that therapists use, which chapter 11 goes over. In the meantime, know that simple, brief, hopeful statements also are good, as long as you also don't dispute or invalidate if the person disagrees with you. For example, you might offer, "There are a lot of therapies and medications you haven't tried yet that might help you."

Take care not to be overly positive and gloss over the person's problems. Stick with things you know are true, not wishful thinking. The aphorism "Suicide is a permanent solution to a temporary problem" helps some people but angers others whose problems aren't temporary. Similarly, "It gets better" is a wonderful message, and it's mostly true. Yet some problems—such as a chronic, incurable illness or the death of a child—can't get better. Rather than saying the problem is temporary or gets better, you could note that change is the only real constant in life. People can experience changes for the better that are unimaginable right now. Love people they haven't yet met. Do things they haven't yet discovered. Cope in ways they haven't yet learned. Get help they haven't yet accessed. These are realistic statements of hope.

Give Information

Be clear that suicidal thoughts are a symptom of a problem, and that problem almost always is changeable or treatable in some way. Let your loved one know psychotherapy and some medications often help people feel better, as chapter 6 explains. Give information about hotlines and other options listed in the resources section. You can also tell your loved one about self-help books for people with suicidal thoughts, which are listed in the resources section. Better yet, you could give the person one of the books yourself.

Offer Support

Generally speaking, connecting someone to professional help should complement, not substitute, the help you give. You can be a listening ear, provide practical support, spend time together, go with the person to appointments, and be there for the person in other ways. Asking the person about their needs shows you care:

"What can I do to support you?"

"What do you need right now?"

"How can I help?"

If your loved one asks for something you can't give, see if there's some other way to help. (If you worry someone's talking about suicide as a way to control or manipulate you, see chapter 10.)

Sometimes, people in crisis can't summon ideas on their own. Just stepping in and doing everyday things to help, like running an errand or doing the laundry, can go a long way, both practically and emotionally. You could also volunteer to help with an onerous task, like organizing your teen's backpack or helping your friend clean out the fridge. Or you could just spend time together and do things you both enjoy, like watching TV, playing video games, or having a conversation about sports.

Encourage Delay

Even when people feel helpless, even when they despair of their situation's never changing, even when they feel too paralyzed to try something new, there's still something they can do. They can wait. In the days to come, your loved one might feel differently about dying. Sometimes, the suicidal wish weakens when a person gets a good night's sleep, becomes sober, connects with others, or does something else that invigorates their body or soul. In the longer term, they can wait to give therapy, medication, or some other healing regimen a chance to work. You might not feel comfortable saying this aloud, but the reality is people can always kill themselves later. Why rush?

One way to encourage delay is the "three day rule." Though unresearched, this stance has helped many of my clients. It calls for making a commitment to wait three days to act on suicidal thoughts—with a catch: if the person feels better to *any* degree during those three days, the clock starts over. Some people have been using the three day rule for years; that's how often their despair is interrupted by hope or relief, even if only for a few moments. The problem with this "rule" is the person might interpret it to mean they should kill themselves if they go three days consistently wanting to die, without fluctuation. Make clear if that happens, you believe the next step is to get professional help or to take some other action besides suicide.

Maintain Connection

People need people. Love and connection, even when abundant, sadly don't protect everybody from suicide. But when they do, they're a powerful deterrent (Zareian and Klonsky 2020).

Connect regularly with your loved one, if your relationship lends itself to that. Check in by text, phone, or in person. Ask how they're doing. See how you can help. You can spend time with the person, write notes, and do other things just to show you care. Try to have fun together. Tell jokes, if that's your thing. Also ask about other aspects of their life besides thoughts of suicide.

Suicidal thoughts—and the problems that drive them—are rarely a one-time thing. They can persist for a long while, leave and come back, or never leave at all. If your loved one's open to it, propose coming up with a shorthand where you can each quickly communicate worry or danger. For example, you might ask the person when you're worried, "Are you safe?" Likewise, the person could come to you and say, "I don't feel safe right now," as a quick way to ask for help. You also could ask the person to rate how they're doing: "On a scale of zero to ten, with zero being not at all and ten being completely, how much are you thinking of suicide today?" This kind of rating scale also can be used to ask the person how much they intend to act on suicidal thoughts. It's one of many possibilities for keeping the lines of communication open about what your loved one's thinking and planning.

If You're Shut Out

Some people who disclose suicidal thoughts stop there. They might change the topic, neglect your texts, or tell you to mind your own business. Has that happened with you and your loved one? It's an extremely difficult place to sit, if so, rife with feelings of powerlessness and fear.

If you suspect or know the person's considering suicide but they won't talk about it with you, consider calling the 988 Suicide & Crisis Lifeline for advice. If you're concerned about your teen, you have more latitude to take them to a therapist, doctor, or hospital for an evaluation.

You also could create a care package. Include a letter or a card expressing how much the person means to you, and why. Say what you value about the person—their sense of humor, their generosity, their moxie. Gather letters and cards from others, too, if you can. This isn't an attempt to guilt the person into staying alive for others' sake but rather to demonstrate that people care. Also, print out information on mental health services in the area and gift the person one of the self-help books listed in the resources section. At least then your loved one will have ways to get help and tools to use on their own. You never know—they just might use them.

This chapter has covered a lot of information. Now it's time to witness brave listening in action. In the previous chapter, you saw how Tabitha worked up the courage to ask her boyfriend, Granger, if he had suicidal thoughts. He said yes. In the conversation that follows, Tabitha listens in spite of her fears.

> *"I'm so glad you told me," Tabitha said. "You must be feeling really bad if that's where your mind is going. What makes you want to die?"*
>
> *Granger grunted, then said slowly, "Because I'm a piece of crap. I'm never going to get better."*
>
> *The thought immediately came to her:* You're wrong. *She didn't believe he'd never get better. But she figured she couldn't change his mind that easily and he might think she couldn't comprehend how bad he felt. So she said, "Tell me more, honey."*

Granger told her how discouraged he felt about his drinking. As he spoke, she listened without judgment. It was hard, but she managed to avoid trying to talk him out of his feelings. Every now and then, she made empathetic statements like, "That sounds so hard," and, "That sucks."

After he explained why he wanted to die, Tabitha summed it up. "So, what you're saying is, your drinking makes you feel bad about yourself, and you feel incapable of stopping, which makes you feel even worse. All that makes you want to die. Is that right?"

"Yep, that's right," he said.

"Well, I think you can stop drinking, honey," she said. "I think you can feel better. I believe in you, but I know it must feel like crap if you don't believe you can do it."

Softly, he said, "It does. It feels crappy."

She asked him how he'd kill himself and Granger said he didn't know. "I haven't really gotten that far in my thinking, to be honest."

"What do you think stops you from going there?" she asked.

"I'm not going to lie," he said. "I think about you, and how much it'd hurt you if I did anything to myself."

"I'm not going to lie, either," Tabitha said. "It'd definitely hurt me, but I also don't want to guilt-trip you. I know this isn't about me right now. What else do you think stops you?"

"My mom, too," he said. "And Pepper," he said of his dog.

"Those all seem pretty important," Tabitha said. "I really want to help you. What can I do?"

"I don't know. I guess you're helping just by listening without freaking out," he said. "I really thought you couldn't handle it."

"Honestly, I'm grateful you told me," Tabitha said. "You can always talk to me. I'm also wondering if maybe you should also talk to a professional or go into rehab, you know? They can help you to stop drinking and feel less depressed."

"Maybe," Granger said. "I'll think about it."

"Okay, if you decide to get help, let me know if you want me to help you find someone or go to the appointment with you," Tabitha said.

"All righty," Granger said. "Wow, I really can't believe I told you all that."

"I'm so glad you did," Tabitha said. "And I hope you'll talk to me again about what's going on inside your head."

After the call, Tabitha felt a mix of emotions. Naturally, she felt sad because her boyfriend was hurting badly and having suicidal thoughts. She also felt relieved to know, be able to help, and feel connected to him when, only a half hour earlier, both felt so alone in their fears.

Bravery isn't an absence of fear. It's doing what scares you despite your fear. You can listen bravely by working from a place of empathy, validation, and reflection. You also can assist the person in getting professional help, which the next chapter covers.

CHAPTER 6

Getting Help

Right after "What do I say?" the question I hear most often from concerned family, partners, and friends of people with suicidal thoughts is "What do I *do?*" Chances are, if you search for information, you'll come upon warnings that "suicidal thoughts are an emergency" and advice to "CALL 911 IMMEDIATELY!" Tens of thousands of websites contain these warnings. Some sites advise calling 911 if someone merely talks or writes about suicide or death.

This is terrible advice. Yes, in general, people with suicidal thoughts should receive professional help, but not everyone must go to a hospital this instant in the back of a police car or ambulance. This chapter gives advice on when to call 911, along with information about plenty of other, less drastic ways to connect someone with help, and obstacles your loved one might face in finding it.

In a time of so many unknowns, when you yearn to know what to say and what to do, information is power. Prepare now to become more powerful.

When to Call 911

Remember, many millions of people seriously consider suicide without being on the verge of killing themselves. And there also are cases of extreme danger, when it's usually necessary to call 911. Here are some examples:

- The person attempted suicide, is seriously injured or unconscious, and needs medical help right away.

- The person feels compelled to obey "command hallucinations" telling them to end their life. These auditory hallucinations can occur in the context of mental illness, drug or alcohol intoxication, traumatic flashbacks, and other problems such as sleep deprivation.

- The person's physically out of control, not responding to your words, and endangering their life or others.

- The person's in so much immediate danger that you can't safely take them somewhere for help. They might flee from you, jump out of the car while you're driving, or do something else that endangers their life.

As you can see, there obviously are cases when the person you love might need help urgently. However, calling 911 can do harm if you immediately go into emergency mode after someone discloses suicidal thoughts without first learning what the person needs right now. Often, it's enough to listen bravely, help create a safety plan (which I discuss in the next chapter), and support the person in getting help later.

Calling 911 should be a last resort because it could place someone in a different kind of danger. The police typically respond to such calls. In one out of ten fatal police shootings in the United States, the police came because a concerned friend or family member called 911 about someone in a mental health crisis (Frankham 2018). Police involvement is riskier than average if your loved one is Black, Latino, or Native

106

American, groups with higher rates of victimization by police (Edwards, Lee, and Esposito 2019).

Thankfully, violence usually doesn't happen, yet the involvement of police can still be traumatic. You can probably imagine why, right? Even in the best of circumstances, police might handcuff your loved one to prevent them from resisting or fleeing. As if the person you care about isn't stressed enough already, they now might be taken to a hospital in a police car or ambulance in front of a crowd of curious onlookers. All this can be humiliating and frightening. The whole experience has discouraged many people with suicidal thoughts from asking for help again.

This isn't to say never call 911 (or another number for emergency services if you live outside the United States). The real message is this: Never call the authorities unless you believe the risk for harm is greater if you don't call than if you do. If the person's life isn't truly in immediate danger, you have other options, starting with calling a hotline.

What Suicide Hotlines Do

In the United States, just as you can call 911 and reach local authorities, calling 988 connects you to the closest suicide hotline within the 988 Suicide & Crisis Lifeline. The Lifeline is a network of almost two hundred suicide hotlines around the country. The Lifeline's original, long phone number remains in operation. Good thing, too, since it was used as the title for Logic's hit song: "800-273-8255." You can also use the chat function on the Lifeline's website https://988lifeline.org/chat.

Suicide hotlines offer support to everybody who needs help for themselves or someone else. It's also fine to call before the situation turns into a crisis. A hotline counselor can coach you on how to help the person stay safe. They can facilitate a three-way call with both you and your loved one. Also, if you're wondering whether to call the police, the counselor can advise you. Here's how the process played out for twenty-two-year-old Miguel.

My brother Arturo told me he's going to kill himself in two months. He said he doesn't want to ruin our little sister's quinceañera, so he'll wait till after that. It didn't sit right with me. After he left, I thought of calling 911, but I wasn't sure they'd do anything. And I didn't know if I should tell our folks. I'm afraid our mother would have a nervous breakdown. So, I called 988.

The hotline lady talked with me about what was going on and gave me advice. She thought I didn't need to call the police now but might if Arturo decides to do something. I asked her if I should tell our parents and she asked me what the pros and cons are. I think maybe they can help Arturo, but I don't want to upset them. Also, he doesn't want me to tell anyone.

She also had information about a mental health clinic near us. I'm going to give Arturo the number. She was really helpful and I'm glad I called. I could tell she deals with these kinds of situations a lot.

If your loved one is in immediate danger, the hotline counselor might end up recommending you call 911 or take the person to a hospital emergency room. The counselor also might call 911 for you. Depending on where you live, another path that hotline staff might take is to call a mobile crisis team.

Mobile Crisis Teams

In some places, when people are unwilling to get help, the help comes to them. Mobile crisis teams typically consist of mental health professionals who go to people's homes—or the streets, for people who are homeless—and conduct a face-to-face assessment. If emergency care is needed, such as hospitalization, the team coordinates that, but their commitment usually is to avoid hospitalization whenever possible.

Mobile crisis services also are a fruitful resource for families and friends who need advice on how to help a loved one who refuses to get help. They're available 24/7 in many areas. If you're in the United States, you can call 988 and ask to be connected with a mobile crisis team, if your area has one.

Mobile crisis services are specifically for people who won't seek out mental health services. If your loved one's willing to go, you could take them to an emergency room yourself.

Where to Go in an Emergency

Hospital emergency rooms aren't just for heart attacks, strokes, and life-threatening injuries. They're equipped to deal with psychiatric emergencies, too. Some cities also have walk-in crisis centers for mental health problems or specially designated psychiatric emergency services that are open twenty-four hours a day. Emergency rooms typically have a security guard or "sitter" stay near someone who's waiting to be evaluated for suicidal thoughts, to prevent the person from leaving or attempting suicide. Some places are locked, so patients can't leave on their own accord. Someone with suicidal thoughts can go to an emergency room alone, come with a support person, or call 988 or 911 for emergency help.

Be prepared. Your loved one might wait hours for treatment in the emergency room. Consider writing in your journal now what you might need to bring to keep both of you occupied, just in case. Think of chargers for cell phones and other electronics, reading materials, snacks, bottles of water, and a comfortable jacket or sweater—for each of you. What else?

Another challenge: While most doctors, nurses, and other health care professionals treat suicidal patients with respect, some respond with hostility. In various studies, staff blame these negative reactions on overwork, burnout, feelings of helplessness, and fear of liability (O'Keeffe et al. 2021). Some health care professionals resent suicidal patients for trying to die when so many dying patients yearn to live. These attitudes can do harm to individuals with suicidal thoughts and their caregivers, as Estelle's experience shows:

> *I took my son to the hospital after he attempted suicide. A doctor was giving him stitches and said, "If you really want to die, do it right and save us the time." I was horrified. Without even thinking, I said, "If you really want to hurt people, get a different job." The doctor apologized, but nothing could make my son un-hear what he'd said.*

Estelle emphatically conveyed to her son that his suicidal thoughts were not his fault and, instead, were a medical problem deserving of respectful treatment. Rude, hurtful remarks typically reflect a health professional's ignorance of mental illness, stress, or other dynamics beyond a suicidal person's control. This gap is the professional's flaw, not the patient's.

Emergency rooms don't provide ongoing care. This visit is a chance for staff to assess your loved one, prescribe medications, and—hopefully, but it depends on the ER—collaboratively create a safety plan and arrange an appointment with a mental health professional. Alternatively, if your loved one requires twenty-four-hour monitoring, the emergency room staff will arrange for psychiatric hospitalization.

What to Know About Hospitalization

The stereotypes of psychiatric hospitals involve gothic, haunted-looking buildings with prison bars on the windows and patients immobilized by straitjackets. In reality, most psychiatric hospitals look like any other modern medical building and straitjackets are as common as rotary phones. Hospitalization can take place in a psychiatric unit in a general medical hospital or a hospital that treats only mental health issues.

Psychiatric hospitalization can be both hard and helpful for your loved one. Hard, because patients lose their freedom. The doors to the outside world are locked from the inside. Patients sometimes are strip-searched on admission to make sure they're not smuggling in dangerous items. At some hospitals, patients must hand over their cell phone, laptop, and other electronics. An aide might stay within arm's length of the person at all times, even when the person uses the toilet or shower. For many people, it's difficult to be away from friends, family, and their familiar bed. Infrequently, in the worst-case scenarios, abuse, violence, and suicide can occur in a psych ward.

Even with these risks, hospitalization has the potential to help. A locked hospital unit is typically safer than the outside world. Patients can't access firearms. Pills are rationed out a single dose at a time. Your loved one might start new treatments, like medication or psychotherapy. Free of their day-to-day responsibilities and stresses, patients can focus on recovery and problem-solving.

Hospitalization can be voluntary or involuntary. If the person's willing to be hospitalized, they (or you) can call 988 or 911, or go to an emergency room or directly to a psychiatric hospital for an assessment. If the person's already seeing a therapist or psychiatrist, the clinician might arrange for admission. Theoretically, people who sign themselves in to inpatient psychiatric treatment can sign themselves out. In reality, if staff believe someone remains in significant danger of suicide, they can refuse to discharge the person and seek an emergency hold or commitment.

If your loved one is unwilling to go to a hospital, you can try to legally force them into treatment. The person might thank you afterward for saving their life, or at least understand why you took such a drastic step. It also could go the other way. For many people, forced hospitalization is traumatic. Afterward, your loved one might be furious and no longer talk with you about suicidal thoughts, out of fear you'll try to have them committed. Those are risks to consider, along with the agonizing risk that the person will die without twenty-four-hour care. Jamal's story illustrates the kind of situation where involuntary care is needed:

My wife, Zara, was gone all night. I didn't know where she was. Called everybody. Family. Friends. Even the police, but they said to wait twenty-four hours. Finally, just as the sun was coming up, Zara limped through the front door. She told me she'd walked all night through a notoriously dangerous area, hoping someone would kill her.

She had this vacant look in her eyes. I begged her to let me take her to the emergency room. She didn't say anything, just walked to the knife stand on the kitchen counter, grabbed the biggest knife, and started to press it against her throat. I grabbed it just in time, but she lunged for another knife.

I held her in a bear hug and called 911. It was the hardest thing I've ever done, but I didn't feel like I had a choice. The police took her to the ER and she was sent to a mental hospital. She stayed for twelve days. Zara was mad at me, but I couldn't just let her kill herself. It's been a few months, and just recently she told me she understands why I called the police. She told me she would've done the same thing if it had been the other way around.

The process of involuntary hospitalization usually starts with an emergency hold for up to seventy-two hours. Those are business hours, so weekends and holidays typically don't count. Many people are discharged well before the time runs out. If someone's admitted for emergency observation, hospital staff will evaluate whether a longer stay is needed. If so, the hospital or treating clinician usually will file applications with the courts, though in some areas, family can initiate that process.

I strongly discourage pursuing involuntary hospitalization, due to the harm it can cause to your loved one, their trust in you, their willingness to seek help in the future, and your relationship overall. But I do need to include guideposts for family members and friends who decide the risks of involuntary hospitalization outweigh the risks of not intervening. You can get guidance about pursuing involuntary treatment from your local police, a Lifeline counselor reachable by calling 988, a mobile crisis team, an emergency room or psychiatric hospital, or a mental health advocacy group such as the National Alliance for the

Mentally Ill. You also can try to collaborate with your loved one's mental health care providers, if possible. Confidentiality laws in the United States permit clinicians to speak with family without the person's consent if there's a life-threatening emergency.

During Hospitalization

Don't expect a hospital stay to resolve all your loved one's problems. On average, psychiatric hospitalization in the United States lasts less than a week (Owens et al. 2019). For many people, this is far too short of a time to achieve lasting, deep change. Hospitals and residential facilities that treat people for many weeks or months are uncommon and, with the exception of publicly funded hospitals, very expensive.

During the hospitalization, you might be invited to participate in family therapy, support groups, or other activities. You can also see the person during visiting hours. I recommend visiting even if the person isn't talkative or doesn't seem happy to see you. Showing up shows you care and helps the person feel less alone. Your presence also enables you to advocate with the medical staff if any problems arise and to give input on a discharge plan.

When you visit, consider bringing things that make the person more comfortable. Call and see what the unit permits. If allowed, you can bring things like slippers, comfy clothes, books, magazines, and photos (but no frames with glass or sharp corners). Anything that could be used for suicide will be confiscated, so avoid clothing with belts and drawstrings. Shoelaces, too. Staff will also lock up belongings that can be used for cutting, like razors, scissors, glass containers, mirrors, and underwire bras.

Don't be surprised if your loved one's hospitalization also helps *you*. Even with the downsides, it can be a relief knowing that hospital staff monitor the person, provide treatment, and maintain a safer environment than what you can provide. You also might feel guilty. Your loved one is suffering, locked up in a mental institution, and wants to die—and you're getting your first night of solid sleep in a long time. It's okay. Take advantage of this break. Rest and recharge so, hopefully, you can be at your best when the person leaves the hospital.

After Hospitalization

The days, weeks, and months following psychiatric hospitalization are exceptionally perilous for many people. The suicide rate is three hundred times higher than average in the first week after discharge (Chung et al. 2019). If your loved one seems just as suicidal after hospitalization as before, it's possible they hid their suicidal intent from others in order to be discharged. It's also possible the person truly felt better in the time leading up to discharge, but then encountered problems afterward that made their mood plummet.

Patients report many kinds of challenges after hospitalization:

- "I thought being in a hospital would make me better, but it didn't. Now I feel hopeless that anything can help."

- "I'm ashamed of having been hospitalized. I should have been able to handle things on my own."

- "The bills for hospitalization have put me further in debt."

- "People treat me differently."

- "Something traumatic happened in the hospital, and it made things even worse."

If your loved one still appears to be in danger after hospitalization, ask them about suicidal thoughts. If necessary, take the person to the ER, call the Lifeline at 988, or in extreme situations when there's no other alternative, call for emergency help from the police or paramedics.

Partial Hospitalization

Some hospitals offer programs where patients attend activities, therapy sessions, and other appointments during the day and return home for the night. Another less time-consuming and more affordable alternative is intensive outpatient treatment, which involves coming to the hospital for several hours at a time, often after school or work. These programs can be used to transition from inpatient care, but they also can be alternatives to full hospitalization if your loved one is stable enough to not need twenty-four-hour monitoring.

Hospitalization is a mixed bag, for sure: potentially helpful and harmful, welcomed and dreaded, and, for you, a source of relief and worry. Whenever possible, it's always best to pursue the least invasive care possible. Most people with suicidal thoughts who receive help aren't hospitalized. They receive care from a therapist, psychiatrist, or other mental health professional as an outpatient.

Finding Outpatient Care

Ideally, your partner, family member, friend, or other loved one already is seeing a psychotherapist, psychiatrist, or both. If so, encourage the person to contact their provider if they have suicidal thoughts or, depending on your role, make the call yourself.

If your loved one isn't already in treatment, you can help them find a therapist, a psychiatrist, or another mental health care provider. For an adolescent, their pediatrician or family doctor is a good place to start for referrals. For an adult, suggest the person ask their primary care doctor. You both can also research providers and mental health clinics online, call the person's insurance company, and ask around for recommendations.

Sadly, many mental health professionals are unwilling to treat people with suicidal thoughts (Gvion et al. 2020). Monika, thirty-four, learned this the hard way when her best friend saw a therapist for the first time. "She spilled her guts and the therapist told her she doesn't accept new clients if they have suicidal thoughts," Monika said. "Oh, and she was billed for the session. What kind of racket is this, where someone trained to treat mental health problems turns people away because of their mental health problems?"

Partly, "defensive practice" is to blame. Professionals fear being sued or having a licensing board complaint filed against them if a client dies by suicide. The system of training mental health professionals also accounts for some providers' reluctance. Most graduate schools in psychology, social work, and other counseling fields offer notoriously little coursework about treating people with suicidal thoughts (Labouliere et al. 2021). Some professionals shy away from suicidal clients because of their own personal experiences or feelings around suicide. These are explanations, not excuses; professionals ought to seek out training and learn to manage their fears around suicide.

If your loved one has options to choose from, you can help them find someone well-suited to treat people with suicidal thoughts. Here are questions to ask in the first phone call, email, or other conversation with the therapist or with office staff:

- Do you treat people with suicidal thoughts?

If the answer is no, that saves your loved one the time and emotional cost of going to an appointment that only brings frustration. If the answer is a qualified "Yes, but…," that's valuable data, depending on what the limitations are. The therapist might accept people who recently started thinking of suicide, but turn away people with long-standing, chronic suicidal thoughts, which can require specialized treatment.

- What is your treatment approach to suicidal thoughts or behavior?

It's ideal if the professional can articulate a specific approach. Too often, their approach is merely to send someone elsewhere. Roughly 20 percent of therapists report that, if a client discloses suicidal thoughts, their first response is to call the police, refer the person to the ER, or send them to a psychiatric hospital (Roush et al. 2018). It's disheartening that professionals would go into emergency mode without first listening and learning if the person actually is in immediate danger.

- What training have you completed on treating people who have suicidal thoughts?

Pay attention here to how much training the person names, if any. Some states require mental health clinicians to complete a certain number of hours of education in suicide assessment and intervention. Especially be on the lookout for therapists who have received training in the Collaborative Assessment and Management of Suicidality (CAMS), dialectical behavior therapy (DBT), or cognitive therapy for suicide prevention, although therapists who haven't been trained in these modalities can also treat suicidal thoughts.

Asking these questions might irritate some clinicians. Those who feel confident about their skills are unlikely to be bothered. Actually, they'll probably understand all too well why someone's asking.

How Psychotherapy Helps

There's evidence that, for many people, certain kinds of psychotherapy specifically reduce suicidal thoughts or the risk of a suicide attempt. These include dialectical behavior therapy, cognitive behavior therapy, and the Collaborative Assessment and Management of Suicidality (Méndez-Bustos et al. 2019). Just receiving any psychotherapy at all—regardless of type—is linked to lower risk of suicidal thoughts and behavior (Calati and Courtet 2016). For adolescents with suicidal thoughts, family therapy also can help (Frey et al. 2022).

In general, therapy for individuals with suicidal thoughts tends to focus on helping the person develop or improve skills in some mix of these key areas:

- Understanding what underlies and triggers suicidal thoughts

- Planning how to stay safe in a crisis

- Tackling problems and unmet needs that contribute to suicidality

- Shoring up hope and reasons for living

- Improving coping and social skills

- Learning to challenge or respond differently to thoughts of hopelessness, low self-worth, and negative predictions about the future.

When an adolescent has suicidal thoughts, family therapy may address conflicts, communication, coping strategies, and relationships among family members.

Medications for Suicidality

Antidepressants, mood stabilizers, antipsychotic medications, and anti-anxiety drugs are often prescribed to people with suicidal thoughts. Two medications appear to directly lower suicide risk: the mood stabilizer lithium and the antipsychotic Clozaril (clozapine) (Hawkins et al. 2021). Other drugs treat conditions that can cause suicidal thoughts such as depression, bipolar disorder, schizophrenia, and anxiety disorders. There's evidence the drug ketamine dramatically reduces suicidal thoughts within hours, but the effects don't usually last long (Siegel et al. 2021).

Paradoxically, antidepressants appear to trigger suicidal thoughts in a small number of people, particularly children, adolescents, and young adults (Hengartner et al. 2021; Hetrick et al. 2021). This risk is considered smaller than the risk posed by untreated depression (Fornaro et al. 2019). Still, if your loved one starts a new regimen of antidepressants, check in regularly about any intensification of suicidal thoughts they might be experiencing.

Peer Support

In some areas, mental health agencies and psychiatric hospitals hire people who themselves have survived a suicidal crisis to offer support to those who aren't yet out of danger. These peer supporters, as they're called, have the added credibility and insights of someone who's "been there, done that." There also are peer-support groups, such as Alternatives to Suicide, that meet face to face or online. Some "warm-lines" are staffed by people who have experienced suicidal thoughts and are trained in providing peer support. There also are other options online such as r/SuicideWatch on Reddit and various Facebook groups. To learn about available peer-support resources where your loved one lives, a good place to start is the Lifeline at 988.

Why to Recommend a Physical

Encourage your loved one to go to their physician, or arrange the appointment yourself if you're their caregiver. The doctor will likely review the person's symptoms and do blood work to see if a treatable physical condition is responsible for mental health symptoms. Shantel's story offers a stark example:

> Shantel, thirteen, had always been what her mother called a "happy-go-lucky" kid. In eighth grade, she suddenly became obsessed with

avoiding germs. She'd wash her hands a dozen times in a single hour. Her anxiety became so intense that she frantically wanted to escape it however she could. She started thinking of suicide.

Her mother took her to a psychiatrist, who asked if Shantel recently had strep throat. Why yes, in fact, she'd had strep about six weeks earlier. The psychiatrist recognized that Shantel had a relatively obscure condition called PANDAS, short for pediatric acute-onset neuropsychiatric disorder associated with streptococcal infections. The doctor prescribed a regimen of antibiotics and steroids. Within weeks, Shantel was back to her old self.

Hypothyroidism, Cushing's disease, and vitamin D deficiency are examples of physical conditions that can lead to depression, which in turn can generate suicidal thoughts. Some medications for physical conditions, such as asthma and epilepsy, also appear to activate suicidal thoughts in some people. Intangible issues like mental illness, pain, trauma, or stress typically account for suicidality, but the possibility of a physical cause ought to be ruled out.

Unfortunately, if your loved one does need mental health treatment, whether as an inpatient or outpatient, they might not always be willing or able to secure it. Let's look at some reasons why, as well as some potential remedies.

Common Treatment Challenges

The mental health system in the United States is, in many ways, broken. There aren't enough psychiatrists and therapists. Services are expensive. Health insurance often doesn't cover mental health treatment as well as it's supposed to, and many people lack health insurance, anyway. Add to these the stigma around receiving mental health care that, for many people, stubbornly persists. These contribute to obstacles you or your loved one might run up against:

Challenge #1: "My loved one refuses to get help."

Many people with suicidal thoughts never go to a therapist, psychiatrist, or other professional (Tang et al. 2022). Even among people who attempt suicide, only 20 percent receive mental health treatment in the month afterward (Hunter et al. 2018). Your loved one is less likely to get professional help than others if their suicidal thoughts aren't severe or if they are Black, Latino, or in another minoritized group (Tang et al. 2022).

People give various reasons for delaying or rejecting treatment, ranging from the personal to the practical:

Personal reasons for not getting help:

- "I'm scared I'll be committed to a mental hospital if a therapist or doctor knows I have suicidal thoughts."

- "I don't need help."

- "I had a bad experience with mental health treatment in the past."

- "I don't want people to think I'm crazy."

- "I believe in handling my personal problems myself."

- "Nobody can help me."

- "I'm a private person."

- "I tried therapy or medication before and it didn't help."

Practical reasons for not getting help:

- "I can't find a therapist or psychiatrist near me."

- "I can't afford it." (Also: "I can't find a therapist who takes my insurance," or "I don't have insurance.")

- "I don't have the time."

- "I can't find someone who has night or weekend appointments."

- "I can't get childcare."

- "I need a ride."

- "My parents won't let me."

You might feel exasperated if your loved one won't get help. Perhaps you've tried to persuade the person, issued ultimatums, argued, nagged, nudged— all to no avail. Chapter 9 gives tips on ways to avoid a contentious power struggle.

Challenge #2: "The hospital sent her home."

In general, psychiatric hospitalization is reserved for people judged to be an immediate danger to themselves or others. "Immediate danger" means the clinician believes the person will die within the next few hours or days if left to their own devices.

Sometimes, doctors and other providers get it wrong. They might not ask the right questions. They might ask the right questions, but the patient doesn't answer truthfully. If you believe your loved one should be hospitalized, advocate for that with the staff. Be specific about what you've seen and heard that makes you worry about the person's safety. If your efforts are unsuccessful and you still believe the person's in immediate danger, take them to another hospital, if you can.

Challenge #3: "The wait is so long."

If the person you love wasn't already feeling hopeless, they might be if they reach out for help and are told to wait weeks or months. Sadly, this happens a lot. The average wait to see a therapist in the United States is five to six weeks, though many people report waiting much longer (Dembosky 2021). When Randy, forty-eight, learned his daughter would have to wait three months to be seen by a psychiatrist, he was incredulous. "How can we wait three months when she might die before then?" he asked.

If your loved one has a long wait, help them identify other resources to use in the meantime. Primary care physicians, for example, routinely prescribe psychiatric medications such as antidepressants. Remind the person about the Lifeline at 988 and peer-support services, and use the emergency room if necessary. Remain available as a listening ear and check in regularly.

Challenge #4: "I'm out of the loop."

You probably know more about your loved one's day-to-day challenges than any professional who sees them only once a week, if that. When it comes to planning for safety, it sure would be useful to talk with your loved one's provider, wouldn't it? This doesn't always happen. Melanie, fifty-one, whose son Darnell has bipolar disorder, says, "I don't know when Darnell's next appointment is with his psychiatrist at the university counseling center. He's nineteen, so they say he's an adult and I'm not entitled to any information. He could've stopped going last month and I'd have no way of knowing."

Confidentiality laws protect the privacy of people who receive health services, including psychotherapy and psychiatry. Therapists, psychiatrists, and other providers can't give family, friends, or others any information about adult clients without the person's written consent unless there's a life-threatening emergency. In many states, for clients younger than eighteen, therapists can tell parents what's discussed in therapy. Be careful. If your teen tells their therapist something and the therapist tells you, then your child is essentially talking to you through the therapist. This inhibits many teens. I routinely ask parents to allow sessions to remain private, unless their daughter or son appears to be in significant danger of acting on suicidal thoughts soon. Most parents have agreed. In the interests of healing, they want their teen to take full advantage of what therapy has to offer, including confidentiality.

Suicidal thoughts are a symptom of a problem that needs attention in the same way that fever and physical pain alert us to illness and injury. This chapter went over different ways you can try to connect your loved one with professional help, and some possible obstacles. Regardless of whether the person sees a therapist or psychiatrist, there are many things you can do to help someone stay safe and to feel better, at least a little. The next chapter covers ways to increase safety, and you'll see in chapter 11 ways to help the person feel better.

CHAPTER 7

Building Safety

If your loved one has suicidal thoughts but the danger's not severe enough to warrant psychiatric hospitalization, the uncertainty and fear you experience can be intense. The world is a dangerous place. There will always be high-rise buildings, cars on the road, glass windows, medications, pawn shops, and other potential accomplices to suicidal wishes. You can't make the world 100 percent safe, but you can try, at least, to make it safer during a loved one's suicidal crisis.

This chapter goes into different options for helping someone stay safe, starting with maintaining a watchful eye on the person, making dangerous items like firearms and medications harder to get ahold of, and helping your loved one follow—or create—a plan to stay safe.

Watch Out for Danger

In hospital settings, patients believed to pose a danger to themselves are placed on "suicide watch." A nurse or aide focuses on watching the person, sometimes every fifteen minutes or so, sometimes never leaving the person's side. You can try to conduct your own version of suicide watch if your loved one doesn't go to a hospital or another secure environment and you're concerned about their safety. If you can, try to organize a rotating group of family members and friends to help you. An informal suicide watch can look different for different situations:

Lauren and Marco were aghast when the emergency room physician said their teenage son Luke didn't need psychiatric hospitalization. They knew Luke was in danger, even if the physician didn't think so. So, the couple took turns staying in his bedroom and the next morning, their son's psychiatrist got him admitted to an inpatient unit.

One day when Luís, fifty-one, phoned his mother, she sounded weak and despondent. "There's no point in going on," Beatriz said. "Nobody will miss me when I'm gone." Luís took family leave from his job, flew to San Antonio, and stayed with his mother for a week. During that time, he got her set up with a therapist, took her to her primary care physician for medication, talked with neighbors who agreed to alert him if they noticed anything amiss, and tended to household tasks she'd neglected.

Marta worried about her friend Daria. She knew Daria was having suicidal thoughts and Daria wasn't willing to go to a hospital. Marta asked if she could stay with Daria to help her stay safe. Daria said yes. Every day after they both finished working, Marta went to her friend's apartment and camped out on the couch. They had dinner together, watched TV, and talked a lot, then had breakfast together the next morning before each went to her respective job. After a few days, Daria told Marta she felt safe being alone and Marta went back to her own apartment.

These are extraordinary measures. In some cases, the suicidal person will feel nurtured, protected, and loved by your vigilance. In others, the person might feel punished, smothered, or angry. If the person insists they're safe, ask yourself if you truly believe the person's in danger, or if you're being overprotective to manage your anxiety. You might have a "don't take any chances" approach in a world that requires taking chances every day. Some people have suicidal thoughts for many months or years. They learn to live with their thoughts of dying. As hard as it can be, you might need to learn this, too.

Remember your limitations. You're not superhuman. You can't be alert to all things at all times. Focus on what you really can control. One thing you can do is to help the person make their environment at home less dangerous.

Making the Home Safer

The acute suicidal crisis—the point where suffering, resolve, and opportunity all converge to make suicide possible—often doesn't last long. If someone with suicidal urges can quickly get their hands on a gun, pills, or other means for suicide, they're in far more danger than if it takes precious hours, even minutes, to get ahold of something. The longer it takes, the more time the person has to change their mind, calm down, get distracted, and stay alive. That's one reason why in the United Kingdom, drug stores don't sell the giant, five-hundred-pill bottles of acetaminophen or aspirin that are sold in the United States. Pharmacies are generally limited to selling only thirty-two pills at a time. After the United Kingdom made these changes, the number of overdoses with these medications went down (Hawton et al. 2001).

So, if you can, lock up or remove firearms, medications, and other dangerous items. Then, if suicidal urges become strong, the person can't turn impulsively to whatever's within reach to end their life. Clearing the home of potential weapons, some of which are everyday items, can be a formidable challenge. Let's look at potential fixes.

Firearms

If you have any guns, rifles, or other firearms in the home and you live with someone who's in danger of suicide, the best thing you can do is store the firearms somewhere else. Adolescents and adults who live with a firearm in the home are three times as likely to die by suicide than those without a firearm at home (Anglemyer et al. 2014). You can store firearms at various places, depending on state laws where you live: possibly a gun club, a relative's house, a pawn shop, or a shooting range. If you haven't already, consider setting this book down and attending to that right now. It's truly a matter of life or death.

If you choose to keep firearms at home, at least make them hard for someone with suicidal thoughts to access. Use a gun safe, a locking cabinet, or another secure area of your house such as a locked basement. You can also install a device that disables a gun, such as a trigger lock or cable lock. Another option is to store the firearm disassembled.

A special note to parents: You might think your child can't access your firearm, but are you sure? Researchers separately asked adolescents and their parents if the young person could get ahold of the parents' firearms (Salhi et al. 2021). In one-third of the cases where parents said no, the adolescents said otherwise. If you're not 100 percent sure your child couldn't somehow get ahold of your firearm, why take the chance?

If the person you love is an adult and personally owns a firearm, then you might feel powerless to do anything about it. Especially in the United States, many people view firearms as central to their protection, their civil liberties, and their identity. Clarissa encountered this challenge with her husband, Joel, who insisted on keeping a loaded handgun in a drawer in his bedside table for security, despite his suicidal thoughts.

Some states enable authorities to temporarily confiscate the firearms of people who could become dangerous in the future. The legal mechanism for doing this goes by different names: extreme risk protection order, gun violence restraining order, or "red flag" law, to name a few. If you want to go this route, your local police will know if it's an option and what the process is, if so.

Clarissa felt certain Joel would never forgive her if she tried having his handgun taken away, so she had a heart-to-heart conversation with him about her worries. Depending on the person's attachment to their firearm, this conversation has the potential to be quite contentious, and I discuss ways to approach power struggles in chapter 9.

If the person simply refuses to temporarily part from their firearm, talk with them about ways to lower the chance they'll use it impulsively. Again, slowing down the process can make the difference between survival and death.

Clarissa tried this with Joel. She asked him to get a gun safe and give her the combination. He said no. She asked him to use a trigger or cable lock. Still, no. So, she asked him to store it unloaded, far from the ammunition. "Look, sweetheart. It's out of the question," Joel told her. "I need to know I can keep us safe on a moment's notice."

If your loved one, like Joel, won't take any of this advice, encourage them to at least put reminders of reasons for living near their firearm, like photos of their children, grandchildren, or pets. You can also suggest a "gun skin" or "gun wrap"—a photo made into a vinyl wrap that goes around the butt of the gun. That's what Joel agreed to. He picked a picture of Clarissa at the beach. Several times in the months to come, this photo served as a reminder to put the gun down—and, ultimately, to not pick it up in the first place.

Other Dangerous Items

Potential weapons and tools for suicide are everywhere you look. Seemingly innocuous items suddenly become frightful—a bottle, a belt, a steak knife. Some people call for "suicide-proofing" the home, but the reality is, it's impossible to remove every potential weapon. Windows and light bulbs are necessities, after all, and both are glass. You secure as many means for suicide as you can:

- Prescription and over-the-counter medications

- Pest control poisons

- Knives

- Razors

- Scissors

- Household cleaners like bleach

- Pencil sharpeners (for eyeliners, too)

- Belts

- Scarves

- Ropes

- Neckties

- Liquor

Don't be deceived into thinking over-the-counter medications are safe just because they don't require a prescription. Overdoses of some common medications, such as acetaminophen (Tylenol) and ibuprofen (Advil), can be fatal. Liquor also can be lethal in large amounts, and it can disinhibit a person, making impulsive acts more likely. Did it surprise you to see pencil sharpeners on the list? The blade inside them is very strong and the plastic ones aren't difficult to take apart. (I hate the thought that this chapter includes a how-to list for people with suicidal thoughts, but the need for you to know these dangers outweighs the risk.)

If you live with someone with suicidal thoughts and they take prescribed medication, hold on to the medication yourself and give the person the required dose each day. It's easier to coordinate this if you're a parent and your teen is in suicidal danger. It's less easy when the person you love is an adult. Ultimately, it's an adult's choice what to do with their medications, so try to present the danger as a problem to be solved together.

Keeping everyday items out of reach is hard. If the person you're worried about lives with you—in particular, if you're a parent—consider buying a small, digital safe that you can keep on your kitchen counter.

That way, you'll still have easy access to knives for cooking, but without the danger. You can find a digital safe online for as low as $30. These personal safes also can be used to store medications, razors, and other items that might concern you. If your main concern is medications, you could purchase a smaller and less expensive lock box. Other options are to move dangerous items to a locked basement, garage, file cabinet, or car trunk, or leave them with a neighbor. In this example, Jiang took a creative approach:

> Before my wife, Sun, came home from the psychiatric hospital, the social worker asked me to search the house and cars for anything she could use to hurt herself. There was so much to secure, I didn't know where to put it all. I ended up installing a digital lock on the hallway closet door. It's a hassle because so many things we need day to day are locked up. A hassle, but worth it, to protect my wife.

Collaborating on a Safety Plan

When people are in crisis, their logical thinking can get derailed. Afflicted with tunnel vision, they might see no way to end their pain or problems. A plan created in advance might save their life.

A safety plan typically involves having the person identify what triggers suicidal thoughts, things they can do alone for distraction, people and places who can help them get their mind off things, people they can turn to specifically for help, and ways to keep the environment safe. In some safety plans, the person writes down their most important reason for staying alive, as a reminder.

Safety plans work. Not always, but often enough that they're considered an evidence-based practice. In studies that tracked people's suicidal thoughts and behaviors for anywhere from three to twenty-four months, people with suicidal thoughts who had created a safety plan were significantly less likely to attempt suicide than those without a safety plan (Nuij et al. 2021). People with safety plans also experience bigger reductions in depression and hopelessness (Ferguson et al. 2021).

Your loved one might already have made a safety plan with a therapist, psychiatrist, school counselor, or other professional. Ask what's on the plan, if so. If you're the parent of a teen, their therapist might show it to you, but the more collaborative you can be and the more empowered your teen can feel in the process, the better for both of you. If your loved one won't share their safety plan with you, you can still have a conversation about things they can do to avoid acting on suicidal thoughts. Then, during a dangerous time, you can ask, "What did you put on your safety plan that you'd do right now?"

If your loved one hasn't already made a safety plan, you can help guide them through the process. The plan can be formal or informal. A formal safety plan follows specific steps and is written down so the person can turn to it for guidance in times of need. There also are safety plan apps for phones. A widely used form created by the psychologists Barbara Stanley and Gregory Brown is available for free at https://www .suicidesafetyplan.com.

Informally, you can ask your loved one what they can do to focus on something besides suicide, get support from others, and resist acting on their thoughts. This kind of conversation especially is useful if the person doesn't want to complete a formal safety plan. Also ask questions about what they can do in a crisis. Later, if they're in danger of attempting suicide, you can remind them of what they might have forgotten. Having a written plan is best, but a conversation is better than nothing.

Staying Alert to Online Dangers

The internet has a lot of good things to offer—connection with others, lots of information, a ton of adorable cat videos—but it also can be dangerous. Social media use has been linked to suicidal thoughts and behaviors, in particular for adolescent girls (Macrynikola et al. 2021). Sites like Instagram and Snapchat can foster snark, competitiveness, and idealized standards of beauty. Some people are bullied or sexually harassed online. And, perhaps most dangerous, some websites offer encouragement and advice for people who want to end their life.

If you're the parent of a teen with suicidal thoughts, talk with them about online dangers they might encounter. You also might want to consider apps or other software that block sites you select or alert you to sites they visit. You'll need to weigh the balance between your need to protect your teen from harm and their need for privacy. Some teens understand and even feel nurtured by their parents' protectiveness. Others respond with hostility and withdrawal.

If your loved one—teen or adult—is frequenting a pro-suicide site, try to learn why. These sites do have some advantages: People can freely share their suicidal thoughts without fear of being negatively judged or committed to a psychiatric hospital. Hearing from others facing similar difficulties can help people feel less alone. Explore with your loved one what they view to be the pros and cons of suicide websites, as well as what they intend to do if they receive destructive advice.

In this chapter, you learned ways to help protect someone you love from suicide. I started the chapter by saying there are no guarantees for safety. The next chapter talks about what to do when, despite your careful efforts to protect the person, someone you love attempts suicide.

CHAPTER 8

After a Suicide Attempt

If the person you love has tried to die, the aftermath is fraught not only for that person but also for you. You might ache with painful emotions: Terror the person will try again. Anger they tried at all. Regret you didn't see it coming or couldn't stop it. All the while, the problems that were present before the suicide attempt still remain, often with new ones heaped on top. It doesn't feel fair, does it?

In this chapter, you'll learn about the potential risks and opportunities after a suicide attempt, ways to talk about what happened with your loved one and others, and the potential for hope, even when things feel hopeless.

After Suicide

Despite the chapter's focus on a nonfatal suicide attempt, I want to acknowledge this reality: while most people survive their suicide attempt, too many do not. If someone you love ended their life, you have my profound condolences. Suicide is a thief. It steals lives with years left to live and it devastates those left to mourn the theft.

There's evidence that grief after suicide can have a different flavor than other grief (Jordan and McIntosh 2011). The *what-ifs, if-onlys,* and *I-should-haves* often are more plentiful, the seeming preventability more pronounced. Self-blame is common. So is anger. Anger at life, at illness, at suicide, and at the person who died.

Amid those excruciating feelings, I hope you'll keep in mind there were forces at play far bigger than you or the suicidal person. Suicide is comparable to a tornado: If high winds carry away someone you love, it doesn't mean the person abandoned you. The storm's forces overtook the person.

It's beyond the scope of this book to go into life after suicide loss, but I want you to know there are resources for coping and healing. Good places to start are the American Foundation for Suicide Prevention's support programs for suicide loss survivors (https://www.afsp.org) and the Alliance of Hope for Suicide Loss Survivors' online forum (https://www.allianceofhope.org). Also, dozens of books address the aftermath of suicide. A particularly helpful one is *Touched by Suicide: Hope and Healing After Loss* by Michael Myers and Carla Fine (2006).

Your Emotions After a Loved One's Suicide Attempt

We expect people to mourn after someone dies by suicide. Grief can come, too, when the person survives. Often, this grief is minimized by others, which Rina encountered with her boyfriend, Alfonso:

> *Alfonso thinks I should just be grateful my daughter survived. He said, "She didn't die. She wasn't even injured." His brother killed himself when he was in high school, so Alfonso thinks I'm lucky. He's right, I am lucky. But why then can't I stop crying?*

Loss is relative. You might mourn because your loved one is in so much pain that they tried to die, or because their suicide attempt created more problems for them (and possibly for you). Another loss you might feel is the "loss of the assumptive world" (Kauffman 2013). Life as you knew it is irrevocably changed. Even if, like Rina's daughter, your loved one survived with no permanent injuries, you might grieve the destruction of your sense of safety, faith in the future, and whatever else helped shield you from the anxiety of an oft-traumatic world.

The stages of grief are well-known: denial, anger, bargaining, depression, and acceptance (Kübler-Ross and Kessler 2005). These stages don't necessarily come in order; they're more like different floors of a building you visit in random order, repeatedly. Recognizing your grief, and giving yourself permission to mourn whatever losses came with your loved one's suicide attempt, can help you make sense of your emotional maelstrom, as Mika experienced:

Ever since Mika's sister attempted suicide two weeks ago, Mika had felt off-kilter. First, there was denial. Mika got the call from her mother: "Are you driving? You need to pull over if you are." Mika turned into a parking lot and her mother told her: "Aiko is in the ICU. She overdosed."

"Oh, she didn't really want to die," Mika blurted out. "It must have been an accident."

Aiko was her baby sister. Seven years younger, she'd always idolized Mika. How could Aiko want to leave her and this world?

In the days to come, recognition of the depths of Aiko's problems came in waves. It hobbled Mika. She'd be race-walking to her car in the rain and suddenly, she'd have to stop, shake, cry. As her sister remained hospitalized in a psychiatric unit, Mika raged at God, at her sister, at herself. Anger consumed her. Other times, she felt so depressed that she could barely move—or want to.

If only she could undo what Aiko did. If only she could take away her pain. She'd do anything to help, she thought—and then realized she was in the bargaining part of grief. Would acceptance ever come? It seemed hard to fathom.

Besides grief, other emotions that often dominate after a loved one's suicide attempt are anger, bewilderment, guilt, and mistrust.

Anger

Are you angry at your loved one for attempting suicide? You're not alone, if so. You might fault your loved one for doing something so dangerous, for frightening you, for seeming to abandon you, for disrupting your own life. This is what Julia says about why she's mad:

> *I spent a whole year planning my wedding. My little sister Jess helped me pick out the invitations, the cake, the registry wish list. And then, the night before the wedding, Jess tried to kill herself. She was in the ICU overnight, we didn't know if she'd live or die, and it was supposed to be my special day. How could she do that to me?*

In some ways, Julia's anger at her sister is unfair. Jess didn't choose to feel so bad or experience so much stress that she attempted suicide. Fairness doesn't always matter when it comes to anger. Emotion comes whether you want it to or not. The next chapter discusses ways to constructively address anger. For now, know that recognizing your anger and not judging yourself negatively for it are a good start.

Bewilderment

Sometimes, a suicide attempt culminates from a long, visible struggle. Other times, people feel blindsided. That's what happened to Eugene, fifty-one. He says, "The day before my buddy Frank attempted suicide, he bought a new fishing rod for our trip to my lake house the next weekend. He texted me a photo of it and said how stoked he was. The next day, his daughter texts me he's in the hospital. I don't understand."

If someone's suicide attempt caught you off guard, you also might fault yourself for not having seen the signs, or you might fault the person for not having shown any. *Why didn't they tell me?* is a common lament. You might question your perceptions. If you were wrong about this, what else are you wrong about? This is one of many treacherous aspects of suicidal thoughts: their invisibility.

Even more bewildering are the whys. Why did the person attempt suicide? Why didn't they ask for help? It's natural to want answers, but even your loved one might not know. A more useful question than *Why?* is *What now?* This is easier said than done, I know, but try not to assign blame, immerse yourself in regret, or torture yourself with what-ifs. Focus instead on what you and your loved one can do now, or next.

Guilt

Life offers so many opportunities for regret, and these become pronounced in the context of suicide. You might regret signs you didn't see, steps you didn't take, things you didn't say. Mohab, twenty, recounts his guilt about his younger sister's suicide attempt. He says, "That same day, she asked me to take her to the mall. I said no. She said, 'I'll die if I have to stay home today.' I said, 'Don't be such a drama queen.' I didn't take her seriously. I laughed, even. How could I have been so dumb?"

As you look back on what you wish you'd done differently, remember that old cliché about hindsight being 20/20. You know the outcome, so the clues seem obvious—now. Not then. At the time, you couldn't know what came next. The worst-case scenario is often obscured by many other, better possibilities of what could happen instead. In Mohab's case, for example, his sister had said "I'll die if I have to..." dozens, maybe even hundreds, of times to Mohab without ever trying to die. He couldn't know this time would be different.

Your inability to read a person's mind or foretell the future is not a failure. It's a tormenting part of being human. Ask yourself, *Did I do the best I could with the information I had at the time?* And if not, rather than dwell on what you wish you'd done, brainstorm what you'll do differently moving forward. Try to forgive yourself for your imperfections. Your pain deserves your compassion.

Mistrust

Maybe you asked your loved one if they were considering suicide and they said no. Maybe they said yes, but insisted they wouldn't act on the thoughts. Consider David's experience with his daughter Rachel:

> *I knew something was wrong. Rachel seemed down ever since she graduated from college. I asked her a few times what was up, and she told me she felt depressed. I asked her—I specifically asked her—if she ever thought of killing herself. She said no. I talked to her about getting help and she said she'd call her physician for a referral to a psychiatrist. I made her promise to call me or get help if she ever felt suicidal. She promised. A week later, I got a call from the hospital saying she attempted suicide. Did she call me beforehand? No. Did she call the physician to get that referral? No. She lied to me. How can I trust what she says now?*

It's painful to mistrust someone you love. It might help to, once again, remind yourself that suicidal urges can overtake somebody without the person's consciously choosing them. Also recognize that people might hide their suicidal intent for reasons that make sense to them, even if they seem illogical to you. For example, they might fear hospitalization, dread burdening you, or hear voices commanding them not to tell anyone.

To repair mistrust, try to have a conversation with your loved one about what made it hard to tell you the truth. Listen bravely. Try to see the situation through that person's eyes.

Some degree of mistrust will probably always be present, even if the person never lied to you. Maybe you don't mistrust your loved one, but you mistrust the suicidal thoughts, the person's illness, the situation, or life itself. Managing the stresses of uncertainty, fear, and mistrust is always a challenge; you might want to look at chapter 3 again for some tips.

What Now?

It's not uncommon for people who attempt suicide to feel anger they survived, along with shame, fear, and hopelessness about their predicament. The problems that prompted the attempt might persist and lasting injuries might complicate the person's life even more. These possibilities make the months following a suicide attempt potentially dangerous (Liu et al. 2020).

At the same time, a suicide attempt can unexpectedly lead to positives. Like the shrill blare of an alarm clock, it wakes many people up to the need for change. It's not unusual for someone to leave a toxic job or relationship, stop substance use, seek mental health treatment, or make other needed changes after a suicide attempt. Their loved ones, too, might recognize changes they can make to improve their relationship with the person. Many people who attempted suicide also report that seeing their loved ones' reactions woke them up to how loved and appreciated they are.

These shifts can bring about growth and healing, though the road to recovery can still be difficult. Let's look at some of the difficulties you might face.

Fear of Another Attempt

It's understandable if you worry your loved one will try again to die. We know that roughly 15 percent of people who attempt suicide make another attempt within six months (Liu et al. 2020). The possibility of another suicide attempt is the bad news. The good news: despite the higher risk, only 3 percent of people who survive a suicide attempt die by suicide in the next year, and the vast majority—between 90 and 95 percent—are still alive many years later (Demesmaeker et al. 2022). Any premature deaths are too many, however, and I empathize with your fear that your loved one will be among them.

Challenges Getting Help

If the person goes to an emergency room after their attempt, they might be admitted to a psychiatric inpatient unit or hospital after being medically cleared. There's also the possibility they'll be sent home, even if you protest. The doctor's decision to hospitalize depends on how much danger the person appears to be in still. Someone who impulsively attempted suicide, expresses relief at having survived, and enthusiastically creates a safety plan with the hospital social worker is far less likely to be hospitalized than someone who planned their suicide for days, expresses regret their efforts weren't fatal, and vows to try again.

If There Are Injuries

A nonfatal suicide attempt can range in medical severity from having little physical effect at all to leaving the person precariously close to dying, with many points in between those two extremes. When a suicide attempt causes lasting physical injury, the effects can be life-changing. Depending on the method used, the attempt can result in blindness, spinal cord injury, traumatic brain injury, or other injuries and losses. Some people need surgery and a long course of physical rehabilitation.

Even with permanent injuries, it's possible for someone who survives a suicide attempt to recover the will to live. When Kristen Jane Anderson was seventeen years old, she lay down on railroad tracks as a freight train approached. The train ran over her and Kristen lost both legs. Still, she has gone on to live a full life, raising her children, running the Christian ministry she started, and sharing her story with others as a message of hope. This is a true story, recounted in her book *Life, In Spite of Me* (Anderson 2010). Her book is quite religious, but it contains universal messages:

Life can get better even when you think it's impossible.
People can find meaning in tragedy.

There is hope even when people feel hopeless.

Not everyone who suffers major injuries from their suicide attempt will undergo positive growth and healing afterward, but one thing is true for just about everyone: You never know. Life, even when it's devastating, can surprise you—and the person you love.

Talking About the Suicide Attempt

Do you feel too afraid to ask your loved one about their suicide attempt? Afraid, perhaps, of stressing the person out, of reigniting painful memories or feelings, of provoking anger, embarrassment, or sadness in some way? In your journal, write all the things that frighten you.

Now write down every reason you can think of to push through your fear. There are plenty. To name just a few: Someone who attempted suicide might view your silence as evidence you don't care or you judge the person. Your loved one might remain alone with painful thoughts and feelings, and you are left alone with your questions and fears. You also miss out on looking together at ways to possibly change, improve, and grow.

So, be brave. Invite the person to talk openly about their suicide attempt. Revisit chapter 5 for advice about listening with empathy, validation, and reflection. Look for ways to help. Convey hope. Check in again.

Also, explore what made it hard to follow the safety plan. The plan, not the person, failed. What changes does the plan need? If the person never made a safety plan, now's a good time. Using information in chapter 7, explain what's involved and see if you can make a plan together.

It's possible, of course, your loved one will decline your invitation to share. Jackie, forty-seven, encountered this when she asked her father about his attempt. He said, "Let's not go there. That's personal." How frustrating! You want to understand, yet your loved one might be too embarrassed, angry, frightened, or private to share. Give them an out. You might ask directly, "Can I ask you about what happened when you…?" Or you could say, "Please, don't answer this if you don't want to. I'm wondering…"

If the person objects, respect their boundary. Say you care and you welcome the conversation whenever, if ever, they feel ready. Your loved one went through something traumatic, and part of helping someone after trauma is honoring their choice to talk—or not talk—about it. In time, the person might want to go there and it'll be easier now that you broke the silence.

Talking with Family and Friends

In a perfect world, it wouldn't matter if others know about your loved one's suicide attempt. It would be similar to your freely sharing, "My partner had a heart attack," or, "My child was in a car wreck." Everyone would respond only with sympathy and support. We don't live in that perfect world yet, so the question of what—and whether—to tell others can add to your stress. It's not always possible to confide in others about your loved one's suicide attempt, but whenever it is, I encourage you to do so. Generally speaking, that includes openness with children and adolescents.

Secrecy can be a privilege you don't have if someone—for example, your children—witnessed the suicide attempt or discovered the person unconscious or injured afterward. Tragically, those scenarios aren't uncommon. When parents do have the choice, they list quite a few fears about telling their children:

- It will upset my kids to know someone they love attempted suicide.

- I don't want my kids to get the message that suicide is a way to try to solve problems.

- My kids will feel rejected; they'll think they weren't enough to live for.

- Knowing the truth will make my children feel unsafe and mistrustful.

- I'm an emotional mess. I need to wait until I can handle myself better.

- My kids identify so much with the person who attempted suicide that I'm scared they'll try to imitate the person's behavior.

- I want to protect my children from harm, and sometimes that means protecting them from the truth.

- My kids are too young to understand.

These are valid concerns. Also valid: hiding someone's suicide attempt from children can create its own set of problems.

Suicide attempts seldom occur in a vacuum. Someone who tries to die usually is also living with extreme stress, mental illness, addiction, or some other hardship. Kids take note when a family member is weeping unexpectedly, sleeping all day, refusing to talk to others, or acting differently in other ways. Like everyone, children crave to make sense of their world. In the absence of truth, they might fill in the gaps with even worse scenarios. If you don't talk about what happened, children's fears can feel like facts.

There's also the chance your children will find out, anyway, or already suspect a family member attempted suicide. If so, they might mistrust you or feel burdened by information they're not supposed to know. They could deduce it's not okay to talk about suicidality, a regrettable message if your children have suicidal thoughts now or in the future. The suicide attempt of a family member or friend is, by itself, linked to higher risk for suicidal thoughts and behavior. Don't panic: the risk still is very small, but if your child considers suicide one day, you want them to tell you, don't you? They're more likely to tell you if the topic's not taboo.

Do you have children affected by your loved one's suicidality? If so, answer the following questions in your journal:

- What are the advantages of your telling your children about the suicide attempt?

- What are the disadvantages?

- What do you think is most likely to happen if you tell them?

- What do you think is most likely to happen if you don't tell them?

- In light of these fears and beliefs, what do you want to do, and why?

Although I think openness is usually the healthiest path, you might decide after looking at the pros and cons that it's just not tenable to share the truth with your kids. That's understandable, too. You're the best judge of what they need and can handle. If you decide to tell your children, here are some suggestions:

Consider Children's Understanding

Very young children don't fully comprehend concepts around death. Use simple, understandable language. You can say some people try to make themselves dead if their mind gets sick or isn't thinking clearly. For older children, the phrases "attempted suicide" or "tried to end their life" usually are appropriate. Most children have learned the word "suicide" by third grade (Mishara 1999). Adolescents tend to know more since many teens already have experienced depression, anxiety, or suicidal thoughts themselves.

Give enough information so kids can understand what's happening, but not so much that you overwhelm them. The younger children are, the less detail you'll probably need to go into. Follow your children's lead, old or young. If they change the subject, go where they take you. Your kids are letting you know they've heard enough, at least for now.

Convey Safety and Hope

Kids look to the adults in their life to keep them safe. Assure your children the person you both love is getting help, if that's the case, or taking other actions to get better. Say you're getting support, too. If they feel hopeless, pessimistic, and frightened, confide in an adult. As much as possible, avoid placing your children in a role of comforting or reassuring you.

This advice to convey hope is harder to follow if the family member's suicide attempt resulted in serious injury or disability. Don't sugarcoat it, but also look for opportunities to be reassuring and comforting, whatever those might be.

Dispel Blame

Many children will wonder if they're to blame. After eight-year-old Emma's mother attempted suicide, Emma asked her father, "Mommy tried to die the day after I screamed at her, 'I hate you.' She did it because of me, didn't she? I didn't mean it, I swear."

Tell your children that even if they upset or angered the person by misbehaving, talking back, lying, or doing something else they weren't supposed to do, that didn't cause the suicide attempt. Listen bravely to what they say, but also explain that sickness, stress, and other circumstances can cloud people's thinking. Directly say the attempt wasn't the child's fault or anybody else's.

Avoid Judgments

If you believe the suicide attempt means the person is selfish, cowardly, or weak, it's better to keep that to yourself, for a couple reasons.

147

One, it's not fair to the person who attempted suicide. Two, your compassion shows you're a safe, nonjudgmental person to confide in if you child ever has suicidal thoughts.

Invite Questions

Like you, your kids will almost certainly want to know more. These are common questions children have about a family member's suicide attempt:

- "Why did Daddy try to die?"

- "Is it my fault?"

- "Does this mean I'll try to die, too, when I'm older?"

- "Is Mama getting help?"

- "What do I say to my sister when we visit her in the hospital?"

- "Is Grandma going to try to die again?"

- "What can I do to make Grandpa want to stay alive?"

Be honest and nonjudgmental when you answer. Use the opportunity to normalize that our minds can get sick or stressed, just like our bodies, and doctors and therapists can help. Give the child space to talk about their fears, sadness, and other feelings. As you know all too well, it's scary when someone tries to die by suicide.

Use Their Imagination

Younger children often work through emotions via play, art, or stories. After you've shared what happened, you could tell your kids a story about someone whose parent, sibling, or other family member tried to end their own life, and ask questions about the character in the story: *How do you think they felt? What questions do you think they had?* Or you might ask the child to draw a picture of what they're feeling. For play, follow the child's lead about what they want to act out and express in the realm of their imagination.

Get Professional Help

A therapist can help you decide whether to tell your children and what to say, if so. A therapist also can help children and adolescents sort through the feelings that come with a family member's suicide attempt, whether you've explicitly named what happened or not. Generally speaking, therapy should complement, not substitute, your own conversations with your children.

Finding Hope After a Suicide Attempt

In many ways, when someone survives a suicide attempt, everything that comes next is a second chance—for both you and the person who survived. It's a dangerous time, yes, and stress and problems can remain intense. There also are opportunities to make positive changes. Opportunities to help the person get help. Opportunities to solve problems. Opportunities to grow and heal. Blake, fifty-six, experienced this change after his wife, Cherie, attempted suicide:

> *Cherie's suicide attempt succeeded in getting me to do something I hadn't been able to do for fifteen years. I'm not saying she attempted suicide because of my drinking. I know it's not my fault. There were a heck of a lot of things that caused it, starting with her PTSD from serving in Afghanistan. But my drinking definitely didn't help.*
>
> *The night she tried to kill herself, I'd passed out in the basement, watching TV. Our son had gotten up for a drink of water and seen his mother. He's the one who called 911.*
>
> *It was a huge wake-up call, really. For both of us. When she was in the hospital, we had a heart-to-heart. Cherie told me it would help*

her get a handle on her PTSD if I got my drinking under control. That night, I went to AA. Got a sponsor. Went to meetings every day. I'm eight months sober now.

It's weird to say, but in a way, her suicide attempt was a good thing. I'm damn glad it didn't end her life. It did end a way of life for us, and this new way is much better.

The weeks and months after a suicide attempt can be quite challenging for both you and your loved one. This chapter looked at the emotions an attempt can provoke, other common aftereffects of a suicide attempt, and ways to talk about the suicide attempt with your loved one and children. In the next chapter, you'll learn how to navigate conflicts that can occur in relation to someone's suicidal thoughts.

CHAPTER 9

Coping with Conflict

For a moment, imagine you're sitting in your living room with someone you love and a stranger holding a gun breaks in, grabs the person, and threatens to shoot. What would you do? You'd probably want to fight the intruder, cajole, plead, make them stop, and do anything you could to protect the person you love. And you'd also probably feel very scared for your loved one and angry at the assailant.

Here's the thing. Someone with suicidal thoughts is both victim and intruder: the victim of whatever painful circumstances, illness, or stress that's taken hostage their desire to live, and also the intruder who could end their life. Meanwhile, you watch. In this scenario, you're unable to control the person or the situation. This tension can lead to many opportunities for conflict:

- Your anger that the person you love continues to think of suicide or has attempted suicide, and your loved one's anger toward you for taking measures to stop them.

- Disagreements about why the person won't go to therapy, take medication, get weapons like firearms out of their home, or do something else you think would help, like exercise, get more sleep, or stop using drugs.

- Your fears that upsetting the person will lead to their suicide, and the feelings of being manipulated that this pressure can create.

- Less commonly, a person's intentional efforts to control or pressure you with the possibility of suicide.

These kinds of conflicts are extraordinarily difficult. You want desperately for your loved one to stay alive, and sometimes you also want to kill them. Not really, of course. But even when you love someone and fear for their life, you can still get fed up, burned out, and pissed off. These emotions pump more stress into the situation—for both you and the person you're worried about.

This chapter goes into anger that you and your loved one both might have toward each other and the situation, as well as common power struggles you might fall into when suicide's on the table. The next chapter addresses the potential to feel manipulated by someone's suicidal communications. Now, let's look at ways a loved one's suicidal thoughts might anger you, using the story of Olga, her husband, Sergei, and their kids:

Olga woke to the sound of screaming on a Sunday morning. She ran toward the sound, and found her son Theo, eleven, bending over his father's limp body on the sofa. Shaking him by the shoulders. Crying. Screaming, still. While Olga called 911, Theo's little sister, Eva, scurried into the living room and started screaming, too.

"Those screams will haunt me forever," Olga tells her therapist later. "I've done so much to help Sergei, and he still tried to kill himself. He's so selfish. He traumatized our kids. I'm traumatized, too. I'm livid that he's hurt us like this."

Are You Angry?

The people we love the most tend to make us the most mad. Our loved ones can push our buttons, impose unfair demands on us, and fail to meet our needs. Worst of all, they can leave. Suicide can feel like the ultimate abandonment. This potential for loss can stir up anger and resentment, especially if the person you love isn't making changes you believe could help.

It's natural, perhaps inevitable in some cases, to feel this flavor of anger when suicidality's present. You can't control what you feel, and anger is a healthy emotion, like any other. The challenge is to prevent anger from harming your relationship. Angry outbursts can alienate the person you love. Also, hostility can impede your empathy and understanding.

Try to understand your feelings and, where possible, defuse them, so your anger doesn't erupt or ooze in ways you don't intend. In chapter 2, you wrote in your journal what angers you about your loved one's suicidality, and how you cope. Now you'll look at other possibilities, too, that you might not already be practicing.

One way to cope with anger is to examine its true cause. There's a saying popular among some therapists: "The person's not the problem. The problem is the problem" (Chamberlain 2012, 120). Reminding yourself of this can summon compassion and patience. Compare these two statements, "I'm so mad at my partner for thinking of suicide," vs., "I'm so mad at the problems that make my partner think of suicide." The second sentence moves away from blaming the person. The problems negatively affect both you and the person you love. You're on the same team. Watch how Olga slowly came to this realization:

> When Olga told her therapist how angry she was at her husband, he gently asked, "Is it possible you're blaming Sergei for something that's not really his fault? He didn't choose to be depressed and suicidal."
>
> "Nobody forced him to attempt suicide," Olga said. "He could've controlled himself."

The therapist shared his view that suicidal thoughts and urges, even when they seem voluntary, usually are the product of problems outside people's control, such as incapacitating stress, mental illness, and hallucinations.

"It's kind of like having appendicitis," the therapist said. "Would you blame someone for that?"

This comparison frustrated Olga. "There's a lot someone can do for that kind of problem, like get help and follow the doctor's treatments," she said. "Sergei could have gone to his doctor and asked for help."

"True," the therapist said. "There are many points where a person with suicidal thoughts can choose different options and ask others for help. The challenge comes when someone's illness or stress hides those options from them or convinces them their situation is hopeless."

Over the next week, Olga mulled over what her therapist had said. At her next appointment, she told him, "You're right. Sergei's not well. If he were well, he'd never have tried to kill himself, especially knowing our kids and I would find him."

Think about what angers you about your loved one's suicidality. Review your journal exercise from chapter 2, if necessary. Take into account any feelings you might have of blame, resentment, abandonment, or hurt. Now, write your answers to the following questions in your journal:

- What are you mad at your loved one about, in relation to their suicidality? Start the sentence with "I am mad at [your loved one's name] because…" List all the reasons.

- What problem do you think contributes the most to your loved one's suicidality?

- How could you name the problem in one or just a few words (e.g., "depression," "the dark moods," "chronic pain")? If you can't identify an underlying problem, you can label the problem "suicidality" or "suicide." And if there's more than one, feel free to name them all (e.g., "addiction and bipolar disorder").

- Now, rewrite your answer to the first question but, instead of using your loved one's name, substitute it with the name(s) you chose for the person's problems: "I'm mad at [name of problem] because...". Then, list all the reasons you're mad at the problem.

- Now, write in your journal how it feels to direct feelings of anger and blame toward the problem instead of the person. Does it feel different? Better? Worse?

This exercise might or might not have helped you. If your anger at your loved one persists, don't worry; we'll address that soon. But if you find some benefit in directing your anger at the problem instead of your loved one, try writing a letter to the problem (or problems). Don't hold back. As much as possible, fight the problem, not the person. Writing in your journal, follow these steps:

- Tell the problem how you feel about it.

- Say all the ways the problem has affected your loved one.

- Describe how the problem has affected you, your family, or others.

- Explain what you'll do (or continue to do) about the problem.

- What else would you like to say to the problem?

Olga wrote a letter to her husband's depression:

Dear Depression,

I'm not mad at Sergei anymore. I'm mad at you. You're a jerk. You tell him he's worthless. You tell him he'll never feel good again. You even tell him we'll be better off if he dies. What a liar!

I feel like you've abducted my husband, and I want him back. You've hurt me, too, and you've hurt our kids. It kills me what they've seen, what they've been through, all because of you.

Depression, I'm doing everything in my power to help Sergei fight you. I'm learning to listen better. I'm taking him to therapy. I'm helping him follow his safety plan.

I'm mad at you, Depression, and I will not give up fighting for the person I love.

Perhaps after doing these exercises, you've discovered that you really are furious at the person, not the problem. Or maybe you're angry at both. Perhaps you just can't know what is due to the person's problems and what is their own free choice. You might also be angry because you believe the person is talking about suicide to manipulate or control you, which I discuss in the next chapter. And your loved one might not have done anything specific but you're mad, anyway. Emotions don't have to make sense.

Soon, you'll look at suggestions for communicating about your anger. First, it's important to consider how you also might anger your loved one.

Your Loved One's Anger

There are many possible reasons why your loved one might get angry at you in relation to their suicidal thoughts:

- You repeatedly ask your loved one to get help, or to take medication, or to stay in better contact so you don't have to worry—whatever it is you want, the person's not doing it and they perceive your repeated requests as nagging.

- You called the police or, as a parent, you took your teen to the hospital against their wishes and they resent you for taking action.

- You watch your loved one more than ever and they want you to stop worrying so much and trust them more. You feel like you can't do enough and the person feels like you're doing too much.

- You text or call a lot, and you panic when it takes time for your loved one to respond.

- You want your loved one to stop thinking of suicide—and by all means, not to act on those thoughts—and the person believes you ought to let them die.

- If you're a parent, you've limited your teen's freedoms in some way to try to protect them.

It can be hard to distinguish between protectiveness and overprotectiveness. Your efforts, while understandable, can cause the person to feel suffocated or punished. Some parents go so far as to remove the door from their teen's bedroom, take away their phone, and refuse to let their teen out of their sight, except to go to school. Even if your vigilance is justified, your loved one still might be angry. Quite angry, in fact.

Many of us are conditioned to believe anger is bad and should be suppressed. But anger's a normal emotion. It comes uninvited, like hunger and rain. Ignoring anger is sort of like pushing a beach ball underwater so nobody sees it. It requires a lot of your energy, and eventually, the ball can shoot out of the water, out of your control.

Rather than stifle your anger or argue with your loved one about theirs, try to communicate about it diplomatically. Here are tips to help you get your message across without escalating anger in either of you:

Avoid Overgeneralization

Remember the cognitive distortions in chapter 3? Another trick our mind plays on us is to overgeneralize. In general, any time you say "always" or "never" in relation to what a person does, you're probably overgeneralizing. As an example, the day after Araceli's husband, Chris, spent the night in the emergency room, she told him, "You always get suicidal when you drink." In reality, there are times Chris drinks and doesn't think of suicide. Not often, but also not never. Chris knows that, and he understandably feels compelled to correct Araceli's overgeneralization. Now they're arguing about the accuracy of Araceli's use of the word "always." Her original concern—the danger that Chris's drinking poses to his survival—has been pushed aside.

A better way for Araceli to express her concerns would be, "I feel angry when you drink because I'm scared you'll think of suicide." This begins nicely with an "I" statement, puts the focus on Araceli's fear, doesn't assume Chris always becomes suicidal when intoxicated, and helps Chris not feel misunderstood.

Listen Bravely, Again

As much as you can, if your loved one expresses anger toward you, hear them out (unless they're being abusive, in which case I urge you to get to a safe place, such as a locked room in your apartment, a neighbor's house, or a shelter.) Be curious, not judgmental, as the saying goes. It's natural to want to defend yourself, but first try to get an understanding of what the person's experiencing, from their perspective. Summarize or paraphrase what your loved one tells you, to make sure you've understood. You might be surprised how much listening to the other person, without rebuttal or dismissal, can help defuse their anger.

Look Inside Yourself

Your loved one might be angry about something you do that you actually could change or improve without betraying your own needs. Maybe the person wants you to listen better, show more of an interest in their life, or help out more around the house. If the complaint is valid, consider making the effort to change. As an extreme example, if you're emotionally or physically abusive to the person, take responsibility, apologize, make amends, and change your behavior. This might mean getting professional help, reading a self-help book, or doing something else to improve. Look honestly at your interactions with the person and see if, and how, you need to do better.

Power Struggles

When it comes to suicide, you and your loved one probably have different agendas. Your agenda is for the person to stay alive. Their agenda is to stop hurting or to solve a problem. These clashing agendas can spark a tug of war, where you both are trying to pull each other onto the other side of an argument. For example, you push someone to stay alive and they push back with their reasons for dying.

If you often butt heads with your loved one about a choice they're making, chances are you've fallen into a power struggle. It's well-known that when people feel pressured by others to do something good for them—like, say, quitting drinking, getting a vaccine, or starting mental health treatment—the pressure can increase their resistance.

A telltale sign of a power struggle is the repeated use of "but" by one or both people. Look out for "but" in this conversation between Gina and her wife, Mariko:

Gina: "Honey, I wish you weren't having suicidal thoughts. I think you should get help."

Mariko: "But I'm not crazy."

Gina: "I'm not saying you're crazy. You don't need to have to have a mental illness to get help."

Mariko: "But a therapist will call the police if they know I'm thinking about killing myself."

Gina: "That's not true. They'll only call the police if you're, like, on the verge of doing it. A therapist will try to help you."

Mariko: "But they'll lock me up in a mental hospital."

Gina: "I don't think that's true, either. Not just for having suicidal thoughts. A lot of people think about suicide without needing to be hospitalized."

Mariko: "But nobody will understand."

Gina: "Therapists are trained to understand what's happening."

Mariko: "But I'm a hopeless case. Why even bother?"

This discussion could go on forever, with Gina struggling to persuade Mariko, Mariko resisting and feeling misunderstood, and both feeling very frustrated. Like you, people who push back probably aren't being difficult or oppositional on purpose. They might truly believe they're right, have legitimate fears it would help to talk through, or feel misunderstood by you. It's also possible their resistance to your entreaties stems from illness or stress. People with depression, for example, notoriously feel hopeless that anyone or anything can help them.

Do you and the person you love get caught in an emotional tug of war? Write in your journal the answers to these questions:

- Where do you and your loved one agree about what you want to have happen in terms of their suicidal thoughts, suicidal behavior, or related problems?

- Where do you and your loved one disagree? That is, what might they want (e.g., to die) that you fear? Or what might you want the person to do that they resist, and vice versa?

- How do these conflicting agendas show up in your discussions?

It's challenging to sidestep power struggles. You can learn from a skill that therapists, coaches, and others use called motivational interviewing.

Motivational interviewing was developed to engage someone in a nonthreatening conversation about possibly making constructive changes, without the person's feeling bullied into it (Miller and Rollnick 2013). Prevention and intervention programs using motivational interviewing have successfully led people to quit smoking, cut back on drinking, exercise more, and manage chronic illness better (Frost et al. 2018).

The premise is this: People usually have ambivalence about their self-destructive or unhealthy choices. That is, some part of them, somewhere, recognizes the wisdom of doing something different, but also has ambivalence about changing. If you push aggressively for change, you can provoke resistance, defensiveness, and entrenchment.

Ideally, people will get in touch with their own motivation when they're free to talk about why they want—and don't want—to change, met with empathy and reflection, affirmed for their strengths, and respected in their autonomy. The motivation comes from within, not without.

In essence, people talk themselves into changing (Miller and Rollnick 2004). That's the goal, anyway. If you use motivational interviewing techniques and your loved one doesn't decide to make the change you want, at least you'll both have been spared the frustration of an unwinnable power struggle. It's also possible you nudged the person closer to resolving their ambivalence about change, which is progress. You'll have left the door open for the person to talk more about their problem, and to make the decision to change without it being a concession or surrender to you.

Motivational interviewing was developed by and for therapists, but over the years, it's been adapted for lay people in many contexts. Anybody can benefit from its principles and techniques:

Resist the Urge to Persuade

As tough as it is, don't lecture, cajole, coerce, guilt, pressure, or plead with someone who's making choices that harm them. Instead, ask open-ended questions to gain an understanding of whether your loved one wants to change, and what they view as the obstacles. Then, listen. Really listen. Reflect. Summarize. Empathize with the other person's point of view, even if you disagree overall. (See: Brave Listening in chapter 5.)

Elicit Change Talk

You can help people talk themselves into changing by asking questions that tap into their desire, ability, reasons, and commitment to do things differently:

- "What are reasons you might want to make a change, if any?
- "What are reasons against making a change?"
- "What do you want to do?"
- "What will you do?"

That last question—*What will you do?*—is especially important, because it helps cement commitment. If the person indicates they will make a constructive change—get professional help, for example, or stop looking at pro-suicide websites—ask questions to deepen the person's thinking and planning, if you can: "When will you do it?" "How will you do it?" "What might make it hard to make this change?" "What will you do if that happens?" Anticipating obstacles now can make it easier for the person to overcome them later.

Respect the Person's Autonomy

The tricky part about motivational interviewing is these questions can just as easily tap into someone's desire to maintain the status quo, their belief they don't need to change, and their plans to keep doing the same ol' same ol'. That's their choice, and it's unlikely they'll make a different choice if you pressure them. You're acknowledging the person's autonomy. Even if the "right" choice seems obvious to you, what to do next is the person's choice in all but extremely limited circumstances, like when someone's involuntarily hospitalized or authorities confiscate firearms under a gun restraining order. If you're a parent, you have more leeway with imposing decisions on your teens, but you'd still be wise to be as collaborative as possible.

By acknowledging someone's autonomy, you help avoid a power struggle and you increase buy-in. Nobody likes feeling their freedom is being threatened. Just about everybody fights to hold on to it. Remember the long game: Your loved one might not change their mind this instant, but you can help lay the groundwork for change to come. The less you pressure the person about their decision, the more they can talk freely with you about it in the days and weeks to come.

These are quite general ideas. Let's put them into action, returning to the example of Gina. Recall that for every reason Gina offered her wife to get professional help, Mariko gave a reason not to. Let's look at the conversation again, this time with Gina drawing from motivational interviewing techniques:

Gina: "Honey, I wish you weren't having suicidal thoughts. Do you wish that, too?"

Mariko: "Not really. When I think of suicide, it seems like a solution, not a problem."

Gina: "How so?"

163

Mariko: "I mean, the problem is I can't turn my mind off. Suicide seems like a way to turn it off."

Gina: "That's a painful place to be. What do you think of getting help, to see if there are other ways to turn off your mind besides, you know, killing yourself forever?"

Mariko: "I don't need to see a shrink, Gina. I'm not crazy."

Gina: "You're worried if you go to a therapist, it means you're crazy."

Mariko: "Yeah, don't you think that's what it means?"

Gina: "I know a lot of people who aren't crazy and see a therapist. But you seem really worried about it."

Mariko: "Yeah, I am worried."

(Gina nods her head sympathetically and fights the urge to talk Mariko out of being worried.)

Mariko: "I'm very worried about it. I don't want people to think something's wrong with me."

(Gina nods again and puts her hand on her wife's shoulder.)

Mariko: "I guess that's stupid because nobody needs to know. And really, if people know, why should that bother me? A lot of people see a therapist."

Gina: "That's a good point. What do you think you'll do?"

Mariko: "I don't know, if I tell a therapist I'm thinking of suicide, they'll call the police and have me locked up."

Gina: "That really worries you, too. Not just being judged, but being locked up."

Mariko: "Yeah, but it's not like I'm really going to kill myself. I mean, if I could feel a little better, I don't think I'd even want to die. Maybe I do need to talk with someone. Do you think anyone would really be able to help?"

Gina: "Personally, yes, I really do. What makes you doubt someone could help?"

Mariko: "I guess my mind is so frayed that I feel hopeless, which is dumb because if I got help my mind might not be so frayed. I could just try it and see if it helps."

Do you see how, by not trying to persuade Mariko, Gina gave her the space to get in touch with her own reasons for and against getting help? Mariko ended up changing her own mind. If Gina had pushed her, then Mariko might have pushed back, held on to her side of the argument, and been unable to see both the pros and cons of getting help.

Conflict, tension, and outright anger aren't uncommon when someone has suicidal thoughts, particularly if you want the person to make changes that they're not making, and vice versa. This chapter looked at how to navigate these tensions. The next chapter looks more specifically at what to do if you feel manipulated by your loved one's suicidal communications.

CHAPTER 10

If You Feel Manipulated...

Fears of your loved one's dying by suicide can lead you to walk on eggshells, sacrifice your own needs, and do whatever you can to keep the person happy and calm, or at least less miserable and chaotic. Consider the following examples:

"I'm letting my son stay up as late as he wants playing video games, stay home from school, skip his chores—whatever he wants. If God forbid he takes his life, I want to know I did everything I could to save him."—Stuart, forty-six

"If I ask my best friend to pay her share of the rent, she has this kind of emotional fit. Twice, she attempted suicide when she was in that state of mind. Now I'm so scared of setting her off that I just pay all the rent myself."—Susanna, thirty-one

"My grandmother said she'd kill herself if I didn't visit her right away. I got there as fast as I could. I couldn't live with myself if she did that because of me."—Malik, nineteen

"I want to break up with Leo, but he says I'm his only reason for staying alive. I feel like he's holding me hostage."—Barry, sixty-three

Making compromises and changes is normal, even necessary, in a crisis. You might miss work or school, give up social activities, or set aside your own needs to be there for your loved one. The person might not have asked you to make these sacrifices. You care. You want to do whatever you can to help. Sometimes you haven't had a choice, like when you've needed to drop everything in an emergency.

Over time, your selflessness and sacrifices can become less sustainable. The more you give up what's important to you, the more you risk feeling manipulated, resentful, and burned out. Has this already happened to you? Take a look at the following list and write in your journal all the statements that apply to you, in relation to your loved one with suicidal thoughts.

- I avoid difficult, potentially upsetting conversations.

  Example: *I'm scared of what my wife will do if I bring up the debt she's gotten us into.*

- I neglect my own needs.

  Example: *I've stopped going to the gym. What if my partner does something to hurt himself while I'm gone, and I could've stopped him?*

- I do things I don't want to do.

  Example: *I went to Las Vegas with my sister, even though I hate Vegas. I didn't want to push her over the edge.*

- I relax rules or expectations.

  Example: *Our daughter was grounded, but I let her go to a party so she wouldn't fly off the rails.*

- I give in on disagreements when I don't want to.

   Example: *I really don't want my boyfriend to keep his shotgun in the house, but he promises he would never use it to kill himself. I have to show I trust him.*

- I stuff or hide my feelings.

   Example: *My roommate would die—literally—if he knew how I really feel about his smoking weed all the time.*

- I cancel my plans for my loved one.

   Example: *I'd planned a dream vacation to Hawaii for a year, but I didn't go because my father said he couldn't survive the week without me.*

- I give gifts to try to make the person want to live.

   Example: *I really detest snakes, but my husband's always wanted a pet boa constrictor. So, I surprised him with one last week, to cheer him up.*

- I've taken over chores and responsibilities.

   Example: *Our son's capable of doing things around the house, but I don't want to add to his stress by asking him to take out the trash or clean his room.*

- I don't ask for help.

   Example: *My wife doesn't know I'm struggling with my own depression. She has enough on her plate to deal with.*

For each statement you relate to in your journal, write how big of a problem it is to you, whether you want to change how you respond, and why or why not. Again, in many cases, your accommodations are necessary. The important thing is to be aware of your feelings so you can manage them without their controlling you.

Are Suicidal Communications Manipulative?

You might notice I'm being very careful to say you can *feel* manipulated, not you *are* manipulated. It's an important distinction because you can feel manipulated even when someone's not intentionally or consciously trying to manipulate anyone. Besides, it's kind of insulting to assume someone's manipulative, isn't it? This stance can block your compassion and empathy. It also can deceive you into thinking the person doesn't really need help.

Outright manipulation does occur at times, and I'll talk about that soon, but very few people who talk about suicide are faking it to influence others (Simpson et al. 2021). They're in pain, or they have a mental illness, or something else is going on beyond their control that gives them urges to die. It's not about you. Any attention or allowances they receive from others is often an accidental byproduct. Think of it this way: a child with a fever might appreciate staying home from school, but that doesn't mean the kid's not sick. Alternatively, the child might be too miserable to care.

You can feel manipulated without someone's asking you for anything, as you can see in this exchange between Sinthura and her friend Lorraine.

At the start of the COVID-19 pandemic, Lorraine lost her job as a travel agent. Unable to find steady work in the years since, she's run out of savings. The other day, she came home to find an eviction notice taped to her door. The only option Lorraine can think of is to go to a shelter, but then she'd have to give up her two cats. That possibility alone makes her want to die.

Sobbing, she tells her closest friend, Sinthura, about her situation while they meet over coffee. "I don't know how I'll survive if I become homeless and lose my cats. If that happens, I'll kill myself."

"Oh, don't say that, Lorraine," Sinthura protests. "You don't really mean that."

"I do," Lorraine says, weeping. "I'll have to kill myself."

Waves of fear overcome Sinthura. Her best friend could die. She blurts out, "You can stay with me."

Lorraine abruptly stops sobbing. "Oh my God, seriously? I didn't even think to ask you because of your allergies. How will you breathe with the cats in your house?"

"I'll be fine," Sinthura fibs. "I can have my doctor prescribe extra-strong allergy medicine."

Lorraine jumps up from her chair and leaps toward Sinthura with a huge hug. "You don't know how much this means to me," she says. "You're saving my life."

Lorraine wasn't intentionally talking about suicide to extract a favor. She didn't even ask. She was stating facts: She couldn't fathom surviving the pain of becoming homeless and losing her cats. She told Sinthura her predicament and Sinthura saw a way she could help. Still, fear, rather than desire, motivated Sinthura to offer up her house.

The tensions between choice and obligation, love and guilt, uncertainty and fear lead to a central truth: just because you feel manipulated doesn't mean the person's manipulating you. Often, the person isn't bulldozing your needs and wishes. The situation is. Fear of catastrophe is motivation enough to do something.

But it's also not so simple. It might appear the person truly is manipulating you. Let's change around the story of Lorraine and Sinthura:

Lorraine tearfully tells Sinthura about her predicament and asks her, "I'm so scared. Do you think the cats and I could stay at your house for a while—until I get on my feet?"

"You know I'm allergic," Sinthura says. "I'd be miserable."

"You could take antihistamines," Lorraine says.

"They make me so foggy-headed. I can't take antihistamines all the time."

"If you don't take me and the cats in, I'll kill myself," Lorraine says between sobs.

Sinthura says, with silent reluctance, "Okay, you and the cats can live at my house."

It sounds manipulative, doesn't it? Lorraine asked for a huge favor, Sinthura said no, and Lorraine then vowed to kill herself unless Sinthura said yes.

Here's the catch: Lorraine still might not intend to manipulate her friend. She could be speaking her truth, from her deep well of pain and fear. She's desperate. No, it's not fair to lay the responsibility for her survival on Sinthura. Maybe in her despair, Lorraine's not worrying about Sinthura's feelings, just saying whatever comes to her fretful mind.

Or maybe she really is exaggerating or even pretending to have suicidal thoughts to compel her friend to change her mind.

Suicidal statements have tremendous power. They get results. If, for example, your teen says something like, "I'll kill myself if I have to go back to school," they're threatening to drop a bomb. And it's not just any bomb. It's a nuclear bomb capable of mass destruction. Your loved one, your peace of mind, and life as you know it could be destroyed.

If someone really is talking about suicide to influence your behavior, that's because people do what works. Behavior is learned, and life is our teacher. Almost everything we do, we do for one of two reasons: We're rewarded by receiving something good, like pleasure, or by avoiding something bad, like pain. The more we do something that brings us a reward, the more we know to do it again. We become conditioned. You might have already learned of these principles, which are called positive and negative reinforcement.

Reinforcement works for animals, too. People can train dogs and dolphins to do tricks for treats. In the case of suicidality, even when manipulation is perceived rather than real, you risk "training" the person to talk of suicide as a way to get results. You're giving "treats." These treats can be things like letting a teen stay home from school or giving in to the other person in a disagreement. You can unwittingly reward your loved one's suicidal communications or behaviors, and they reward your reactions by staying alive. Your loved one does what works, and you do, too.

In the following example, see if you think conditioning could be occurring:

After Ruth, sixteen, attempted suicide, her horrified parents stood by her hospital bed and asked her why. "I don't have anything to live for," Ruth said. "I don't have anything to look forward to."

"What can we do to help?" her mother, Tova, asked.

Ruth stared at the ceiling while she considered the question. She turned to her parents and said, "You could get me a puppy."

The next weekend, after Ruth was discharged from the hospital, her parents took her to an animal shelter and Ruth picked out their new family member. The puppy had a dramatic effect on Ruth's mood. It gave her a reason to wake up, to exercise, to laugh. The medication and therapy also helped, and soon, Ruth no longer wanted to die.

She relapsed a few months later. Attempted suicide again. Ended up in the hospital again. Her mother, again, asked what could help. "A car," Ruth said. "I'd feel better if I could drive myself places when I wanted to."

The weekend after Ruth's discharge, her parents took her to pick out a new car.

Was Ruth manipulating her parents? It's complicated. It would be manipulative if she was pretending to think of suicide in order to get her needs met. Otherwise, her truth merely converged with her parents' generosity and concern. However, Ruth is also learning from these experiences that her parents grant her wish when her life is at stake. This kind of reinforcement can be pronounced if gifts, care, and attention flow *only* when she expresses suicidal thoughts.

Still, whether your generosity reinforces suicidal communications or not, there are times you need to accommodate your loved one's needs or wishes without worrying about reinforcement, for two reasons:

reinforcement shouldn't always be avoided, and reinforcement isn't always avoidable.

Reinforcement Shouldn't Always Be Avoided

You want to reward suicidal communications at least a little, don't you? If you react with skepticism, irritation, or judgment when your loved one discloses suicidal thoughts, the instinct to avoid punishment might deter the person from confiding in you again. Responding with compassion can reinforce the behavior you want the person to continue.

Reinforcement Isn't Always Avoidable

If someone's in crisis, the risk of reinforcement pales in comparison to the possibility of death. Never withhold something important your loved one needs only because you fear being manipulated. The harm of ignoring your loved one's suicidal danger outweighs the potential harm of conditioning. Your challenge is to be mindful of when your actions might be reinforcing and what you can do to mitigate those effects.

Responding to Perceived Manipulation

There is no one "right" thing to do if you sense your loved one talks of suicide to influence or coerce you. Like one of those "choose your adventure" books, a single word or statement can send your conversation down a unique path. It's impossible to predict what comes next. With that said, here's advice to hold in mind:

Take Suicidal Statements Seriously

It's not necessarily *either/or* when it comes to whether someone truly is considering suicide or they're trying to influence you. Sometimes, it's *both/and:* the person's sincere about their suicidal wishes *and* leveraging your feelings of fear, concern, and obligation.

So, if you believe someone's talking about suicide only to get you to say or do something they want, still presume the danger is real. Ask yourself, *If what this person says is true, how would my response help or hurt?* Don't discount someone's pain or distress. If in doubt, it's better to err on the side of believing someone who's being disingenuous rather than disbelieving someone who intends to end their life.

Connect with Compassion and Empathy

It can be infuriating to feel manipulated. It might help to remind yourself that, if your loved one is trying to influence you, the person's almost certainly doing so because they're in pain or have some other unmet need. Pain avoidance is an instinct. People tend to do the best they can. Don't expect people to use problem-solving or communication skills they simply don't have yet. This is especially true of adolescents, as Ben and Elijah's story shows:

Standing in the doorway of his son Elijah's bedroom, Ben announced it was time to get ready for church. A football player on his middle school team, Elijah wanted to sleep late the morning after a big game. His father said no.

"I swear I'll kill myself if you make me go to church," Elijah screamed, still lying under the covers.

Ben walked to Elijah's bed, sat down on the edge, and said, "Oh, that's serious, buddy. What's going on?"

Elijah was stunned. He'd expected his dad to say, "Okay, okay, you don't have to go to church." Not to get that soft tone of voice he used whenever he was concerned. But Elijah also didn't want to admit he didn't mean it.

"I'm really worried about you," Ben said. "Let's talk about what's going on that makes you want to die."

Uh-oh, *Elijah thought. This is getting out of hand. He sat up in bed. "Um, Dad, I don't really want to kill myself. I just said it to show you how mad I am."*

"Well," his dad said, "that's a relief you're not in danger. Let's talk about other ways you can get that point across. If you tell me you're going to kill yourself, I'll take action to protect you."

"Sorry," Elijah said.

"I'm glad we're talking about this. What's a different way you can tell me how important something is to you, or how angry you are?"

"I guess I could say, 'Dad, I don't think you understand what a big deal this is for me. I'm really mad.'"

"Right," Ben said. "It's better to tell me your feelings than to threaten suicide. I'll take you to the ER in a heartbeat if you're in danger, but if you say you want to kill yourself just to show me how angry you are, it's better to tell me you're angry."

"True," Elijah said, and he got out from under the covers to get ready for church.

Focus on Next Steps

Instead of addressing the person's request or demand right away, prioritize keeping the person safe. You saw Elijah's dad do this. He asked his son to tell him what's going on, rather than focusing on Elijah's request to skip church. If Elijah continued to say he would kill himself, his father could listen and decide what help was needed. Maybe suicidal urges really did come to Elijah when he thought of going to church. If so, the problem to be tackled isn't the pesky family rule about church. Instead, the problem is Elijah's emotional dysregulation, specifically his inability to handle disappointment.

An important exception to this advice: if you're trying to end a relationship and the other person tells you they'll die by suicide if you leave, now's not a good time to have a long discussion about their safety, particularly if the person's been abusive or controlling with you. That kind of negotiation keeps you connected. In the worst-case scenario, giving in to this pressure traps you in a dangerous situation. (More on that soon.)

Stick to Your Limits

Many people, especially parents, change their expectations when someone they love has suicidal thoughts. Sometimes this is unavoidable. You wouldn't expect someone with a broken leg to run around the block. Along the same lines, expecting someone debilitated with, say, depression, to do work around the house might be just as formidable. But if the person is capable of doing what's expected or needed, I recommend not making a habit of bending rules, lowering expectations, or hiding your needs and feelings only out of fear.

Let's return to the example of Ben and his son Elijah. If Ben acquiesced and let Elijah stay home from church, that would give Elijah relief in the short term. In the long term, it would send the message that suicidal communications will succeed in getting a rule relaxed. The cycle likely would happen again many times—the son's demand, his father's acquiescence, the coercive behavior's reinforcement. Instead of learning how to manage his emotions, Elijah would learn how to get his dad to bend the rules.

Sometimes, maintaining limits can be terrifying. What if someone who seemingly gives you an ultimatum really will try to end their life if you refuse? That's why it's wise to proceed as if the danger is real. Listen, learn more about your loved one's suicidal thoughts, and explore what they need to do next. They might need to use their safety plan or go to an emergency room. That way, your focus remains on the person's safety while you also assert your needs. And if they aren't truly in danger, they learn that threatening suicide isn't a ticket to your dropping limits and expectations.

Get Professional Help

If you've become entrenched in a pattern of accommodation and reinforcement because you fear your loved one will die, it can be hard to extricate yourself. Especially at first, your feelings of fear and guilt might constrain you from doing something different. And, if you halt a pattern of reinforcement that the person has become used to, they could ramp up their threats, at least temporarily, to prove you need to gratify them. A therapist can guide you through the process of learning new communication skills, asserting yourself while helping your loved one, and more. For adolescents, family therapy can equip everyone with skills to maintain boundaries, stick to limits, and resist manipulation while also not losing sight of the person's problems, pain, and need for empathy.

If You Want to Leave...

It can be daunting to end a relationship with someone who says they'll literally die without you. You want to leave, but you also don't want the person to die, and you don't want to feel responsible if they do. The uncertainty about their true danger can make your unease even worse. If you feel you must help, try to stick to the person's safety plan (or help create one, if you're safe and willing to do so). If you must leave right away, leave. You can notify somebody about the person's danger, like the person's friends or the police.

The advice to recognize your boundaries and stick to your limits is even more relevant if the person might harm you physically. Coercive suicide threats can be part of a pattern of intimate partner violence, such as physically or emotionally abusing you, trying to control your life, and reacting with jealousy, suspicion, and possessiveness. If your partner's suicidal statements seem to be a larger pattern of abuse and control, please get help. Your life could be in danger. In the United States, call the National Domestic Violence Hotline at 1-800-799-7233 (SAFE) or text 88788. You can also chat with someone online through the hotline's website at https://www.thehotline.org.

It's not selfish to end a relationship. Even if the person carries out their suicide threat, it doesn't mean you're to blame. You need and deserve to take care of yourself, both physically and emotionally. Giving in to emotional blackmail will only bind you to someone for all the wrong reasons. A healthy relationship is based on love, not feelings of fear, coercion, obligation, or guilt.

This chapter started with stories of people who felt manipulated by their loved one's suicidal communications. To illustrate what you've learned here, here are potential responses to each scenario.

Son: "If you really wanted me to stay alive, you'd let me do whatever I want, not make me follow your stupid rules."

Fear-based response: "Of course, I want you to stay alive. It's fine—you can keep playing your video games tonight."

Assertive response: "If you're thinking of killing yourself, I want to help you feel better and get help. First, what are your suicidal thoughts?"

Friend: "How can you expect me to pay rent and help around the apartment when you know I might kill myself?"

Fear-based response: "You're right. Your life is more important than anything. I'm sorry I asked."

Assertive response: "I hate that you're struggling, but it's not fair to put everything on me. We need to make a plan for how you can help out, but first, what do you need now to stay safe?"

Grandmother: "What's the point of living if you won't visit me right now? I might as well kill myself."

Fear-based response: "I'll cancel my plans and come over."

Assertive response: "That's so sad. I can't visit right now, so let's talk about what you can do to be safe. I love you, and I don't want you to die."

Boyfriend: "Honey, if you leave me, I'll kill myself."

Fear-based response: "I'm sorry. I'll stay."

Assertive response: "I want you to stay alive, but I can't be responsible for your life. I think you should call the suicide hotline or go to an emergency room."

You can see that the assertive responses, like Ben's approach earlier with his son Elijah, don't focus on the person's requests. Instead, the responses assert a boundary and focus on the person's safety. This approach doesn't resolve all ambiguity and fear you might face in these challenging situations. That's impossible. You'll still need to take into account all the unique aspects of your situation. Sometimes, you might decide it's better for the person to use their safety plan or do something else that empowers them to learn and change. Other times, you might decide to help the person any way you can, no matter what.

The potential for manipulation is complicated. I want to reiterate that you might feel manipulated because of the situation's urgency, not someone's conscious, intentional coercion. There are times, though, when people do invoke suicide to control or shape others' actions. It's very hard to know what someone's true motives are. If you're in doubt, assume the danger is real and focus on ways the person can get help and stay safe.

CHAPTER 11

Fostering Hope

So far, we've looked at ways to help your loved one stay alive while also tending to your own needs. Survival, by itself, is seldom enough. You also want the person to *want* to survive, don't you? This means trying to help the person feel better, solve their problems, and feel hopeful, if you can. But how? You're not your loved one's therapist. You're not their psychiatrist, nurse, or pharmacist, either. Instead, you're their parent, partner, friend, or someone else who cares.

As it turns out, you don't need training as a therapist to borrow some therapy tools. This chapter goes over techniques you can use to help your loved one identify reasons for living, tackle problems that drive their suicidal thinking, and rediscover hope.

First, let me make a few things clear. In this chapter, I draw from evidence-based treatments, expert guidance, and my own clinical practice, but I can't promise these tools will work for everyone. Believe me, I wish I could. Check in with your loved one about whether your efforts are helping and what you could do that might help more. Also, the conversations I propose below are seldom useful when someone's in crisis. If your loved one's in immediate danger, seek emergency help as described in chapter 6.

Beware of a power struggle. You learned in chapter 5 to listen bravely without immediately trying to change what you're hearing. Once you've truly listened, trying to instill hope is less likely to short-circuit the conversation and leave your loved one feeling alienated. Still, return to listening and reflecting if you find yourself trying to convince your loved one to do something and they're resisting. As much as possible, try to help people uncover their own reasons for staying alive, rather than trying to persuade them.

And remember, even though this chapter describes ways to try to foster hope, you don't always have to *do* anything. Sitting with someone who's hurting and bravely listening without judgment, interruption, or a fix-it attitude are sometimes the most powerful tools of all.

Now, let's look at what helps many people with suicidal thoughts survive—and more.

What Stops People from Suicide?

Every now and then, someone asks on the discussion website Reddit, "What stopped you from killing yourself?" A group of researchers pored over six thousand responses and looked for recurring themes (Mason et al. 2021). Here are the main things that deterred people from acting on their suicidal thoughts, in order of frequency:

Friends and Family

People cited friends and family as reasons for living four times more often than the next most popular reason. Not only did people say they wanted to protect their loved ones from the grief and pain of a suicide loss but they also didn't want to burden others with cleaning up their apartment or finding their body.

Curiosity and Optimism

Life is a book whose plot we discover day by day, without knowing where it will take us or how it will end. Some people stay alive for this reason. "I kinda want to see what happens next," one person shared in the Reddit comments.

Spite

It might surprise you to see "spite" make the list of reasons for living, especially so high. But it also makes sense, when you consider the saying, "Living well is the best revenge." One person wrote, "I don't want my haters to win."

Purpose in Life

Some people live to fulfill responsibilities, projects, and goals, like raising children or finishing a thesis. This motivation is reminiscent of the Robert Frost poem "Stopping by Woods on a Snowy Evening," which some critics say is about suicide (Monteiro 2002):

The woods are lovely, dark and deep
But I have promises to keep,
And miles to go before I sleep,
And miles to go before I sleep.

Transience

Feelings change. So do thoughts, relationships, situations, and problems. One person in the Reddit study summed it up like this: "With time, the thing causing me pain will pass. Everything does."

Hobbies

Some people said they didn't end their life at least partly because of their love for books, music, video games, and sports. Others cited things like masturbation and porn. Whatever activities give someone pleasure can be, by themselves, reasons for living.

Pets

Pets oblige their people to get out of bed—and to keep doing so. The dog needs a walk. The cat needs food. Psychotherapy clients have told me they're daunted by the possibility their cats or dogs would go to a shelter, where they'd be caged, traumatized, and possibly euthanized. "My dog needs me," someone wrote in the Reddit study.

Fear

The possibility of surviving a suicide attempt with permanent injuries is enough to stop some people. Others want to avoid the shame and judgments that they feel certain would come if they tried to die, but lived. People also might worry about a painful dying process or worse pain in an afterlife. Or they fear taking irreversible action to kill themselves and then regretting it in their final moments of consciousness.

Lack of Energy or Motivation

For some people with suicidal thoughts, it's easier just to go to sleep, even though that means waking up again. Inertia is a powerful force. "I'm too lazy/apathetic to actually stop doing the living thing," one person said on Reddit, echoing the responses of hundreds of others.

Intervention by Others

A shout to a stranger on a ledge. A door opening while someone swallows pills. These interruptions often are life-saving. One person recounted on Reddit that a stranger yelled, "Get down from there!" as the person prepared to jump. "This caused me to snap back to reality and I ran for my car," the person wrote.

Medication, and More

Some people credited medications with saving their life. Others credited their survival to going to psychotherapy, not having a firearm in the house, or having nightmares about the suicide attempt and its possible consequences.

Those are some things that stop others from succumbing to suicidal urges, but the most important thing for you to know is what stops your loved one. I recommend finding out. You can ask the person, "What's stopped you from acting on your suicidal thoughts?" A related question to ask and explore is, "What are your reasons for staying alive?"

This advice scares some of my students. They see it almost as a dare, as if they're saying, "If you really wanted to kill yourself, you would have done it already. What stops you?"

In reality, you're merely saying aloud what many suicidal individuals constantly ask themselves: Why live? And people with suicidal thoughts who don't ask themselves that question might find it useful. The answers can illuminate for them reasons to stay alive.

Janet, thirty-one, tried both these questions with her mother, Lydia:

Mom was telling me all the reasons why she should kill herself. I told her, "It seems like you're pretty clear about why you should die. I'm by no means suggesting you kill yourself, but I am curious to know what's helped you to keep going this long."

She said she's afraid she'll go to hell, or she'll do something that makes her situation even worse, like if she attempts suicide and is paralyzed or brain-damaged. But then she started saying other things, too, like that she wants to know her grandchildren when I have kids. It was amazing to hear her talk about the future in any kind of positive way.

As a psychotherapist, I've observed that deterrents to suicide tend to fall into two categories: hope and fear. Hopes for the future keep many people alive, as do fears about what will happen if they die—or try to. You can borrow from therapy techniques to strengthen motivation to live, awaken hope, and leverage fears. Let's look at some possibilities.

Tap into Ambivalence

Invite your loved one to share the pros and cons of suicide. Like the motivational interviewing techniques you read about in chapter 9, this kind of conversation can create the space for them to argue with themselves, not you, about whether to live or die. Like the other ideas presented here, looking at reasons for and against suicide can also help people broaden their perspective.

If you worry your questions could make it seem you support suicide, you could first say something like, "Obviously, I don't think suicide is the right choice for you, but I want to see things from your perspective." And then, "So, what, for you, are the biggest reasons to die by suicide, and the biggest reasons to live?" Another way to frame this is to ask the person, "What does the part of you that wants to die say, and what does the part that wants to live say?" These questions normalize the inner, often incessant arguments that accompany suicidal thoughts.

Examine Fears

Some people can't muster one iota of hope. Only fear keeps them alive—fear of dying, of surviving a suicide attempt with worse injuries, of suffering a worse fate in an afterlife, of harming others with their death.

Just as it's better not to impose reasons for hope on people, the same is true with fear. Rather than tell your loved one what should frighten them, you can help them connect with their own fears by asking non-judgmentally, "What scares you about trying to kill yourself?"

Janet was touched by her mother's answer to that question. "She told me she's scared she'll never make her way back to my dad because he's in heaven and she's scared she'd go to hell," Janet said. "I wouldn't feel right threatening my mother with hell if she kills herself. But if she wants to say that to herself and it stops her from ending her life, that's fine by me."

Share Cognitive Tools

You read in chapter 3 about ways to identify cognitive distortions that add to your distress, talk back to your thoughts, and practice mindful observation when you just can't change your thoughts and feelings. These tools can help your loved one, too, if you'd like to share them. They draw mostly from cognitive behavior therapy, which research has found can reduce suicidal thoughts, suicide attempts, and hopelessness (Wenzel and Jager-Hyman 2012).

Search for Strengths

It's fine to tell your loved one you believe they can get through this hard time. It's even better to help the person recognize and believe it, based on their past experiences. Asking your loved one questions about other tough times can help them identify strengths they might have lost sight of. Janet tried this with her mother:

She was saying how lonely she is, how she feels like she doesn't have any sort of purpose on earth. I asked her, "Have you ever felt this way before, Mom?" She said, "Yes, about ten years ago, right after your dad died, I went through a spell of wanting to kill myself." I asked her, "What helped you get through that dark time?"

She kind of had this aha moment. Years ago, she'd spent time volunteering in the church nursery every Sunday. Somehow, she'd forgotten how much it helped to be around the babies and kids. Now she said she's going to try to do that this Sunday.

It's not surprising that Janet's mother forgot what helped her years earlier. Researchers have documented that people with suicidal thoughts often are unable to summon good memories (Ellis 2006). Remember the tunnel vision that suicidality can cause? Well, it's a very dark tunnel, and darkness obscures vision. Not always, but sometimes, exploring what's worked in the past can help turn on the light.

Look at Unfinished Business

Hope involves goals and plans—not only goals to feel better but also places to see, things to do, and projects to finish. Reaching goals takes time, and time is a wedge between suicidal thoughts and action. The bigger that wedge, the better. Help your loved one identify reasons to delay suicide by asking, "What do you want to see, do, and finish while you're alive?"

This is an "unfinished business" list (Ellis and Newman 1996). Try to get as many ideas churning as possible—TV shows to watch, tattoos to get, foods to try. Every idea is a reason to "procrastinate" suicide, buying more time. Janet's mother, Lydia, mentioned future grandchildren. Janet wanted to see if she hoped for other things, too:

I asked Mom, "What are things you've always wanted to do before you die?" Without any hesitation at all, she said, "See the Pacific Northwest." She'd never gone. We live in New Hampshire, but it's doable. It's like she couldn't see possibilities anymore. I guess that just shows how bad she's been feeling. She mentioned other things, too. Like, she's always wanted to learn to knit and to volunteer at an animal shelter. I wrote down all her unfinished business so I can remind her if she forgets.

Suggest a Hope Box

Many therapists invite clients to collect tangible reminders of things to hope for, as part of an evidence-based treatment for suicidal thoughts (Wenzel et al. 2009). The potential rewards are two-fold: gathering items for the hope box often is therapeutic and, later, if the person's mood worsens, going through the hope box can help counter hopelessness.

Just about anything that has meaning to the person can go in the hope box. In my practice, some things consistently turn up: photos of people and pets they love and places they hope to visit; birthday cards and printed emails that hold special meaning; and favorite quotations, poems, and song lyrics. Some people like to decorate their box and make an art project of it. There also are mobile apps, such as the Virtual Hope Box, to keep photos, screenshots, and songs in one place.

You could suggest a hope box to your loved one, help them brainstorm what to put into it, and even assist in putting it together if the person's game. That's what Janet did with her mother:

At first, Mom couldn't think of anything to put in it, so I got out the unfinished business list. The next day when I saw her, she had a box filled with things like photos of the Oregon coastline that she'd printed from the internet, a pair of knitting needles, and a favorite cookbook. She even went into the basement and got a pair of my old baby shoes she'd saved, as a reminder that she might be a grandma soon.

Evoke Future Selves

Visualizing life in the years to come can, in many cases, help people think beyond their current distress (Wenzel and Jager-Hyman 2012). Ask your loved one to imagine what they'll be like a year from now. Two years. Five years. Not only different times, but also different roles: spouse, parent, worker, retiree, great grandparent, and so on. If the person you're concerned about is an adolescent, you could ask them to envision living in another city, getting their first pet as an adult, or going to college if that's in their plans. By considering their future selves, people can step outside the rigid, habitual, narrowed thinking that comes with suicidality. Janet witnessed this shift with her mother:

> It was a dangerous question for me to ask: can you imagine yourself five years from now? My mom's sixty-eight. She was rattling off all the health problems she could have over the next five years. But then she started coming up with other things, too, like that she wants to move into a senior community, where they have social activities and she'd be with other widows. So, I asked her to imagine what life might be like five years from now in the independent living place near my house. At the very least, it gives her something to think about besides suicide.

Your loved one might see only more suffering to come, and nothing else. This reveals a dangerous level of hopelessness and it underscores the need for professional help. Hopefully, the person can at least imagine life's changing, even if they don't believe it will.

Problem-Solve Together

Ultimately, to many people with suicidal thoughts, suicide solves problems. Try to see it from their eyes: As far as we know scientifically, death ends physical and emotional pain. Almost always, other possible solutions exist, but the person can't see them. Raise this possibility: "If you could solve your problems another way, would you still want to die?" People tend to answer along the lines of, "No, of course not!" They don't exactly want to die. They want their problems, pain, or existential malaise to cease.

The challenge is that many people become suicidal precisely because they lack good problem-solving skills (Ellis 2006). This makes "only" a dangerous four-letter word, as in, "Suicide is the only solution" (Shneidman 1996, 59).

Methodically thinking through problems, setting goals, and taking action can counter this myopia. To do this, you can guide your loved one through the problem-solving method, which breaks the process down into five steps (Nezu et al. 2015):

1. Identify the biggest problems.

2. Consider all possible options for solving the problem.

3. Evaluate the pros and cons of each option.

4. Select and try out an option.

5. Evaluate results.

You can help at each stage. Share what you've observed that contributes to the person's situation. Invite the person to brainstorm as many ideas as possible—even bad ones. The more ideas, the better. There is no "good" or "bad" when it comes to brainstorming. Now, ask about the pros and cons of every option. That includes suicide, if you haven't asked already. Encourage the person to select an option to try first. If they're unable or unwilling to try any alternatives to suicide, emergency help might be needed.

Once your loved one has decided what to try, help the person put their proposed alternative into action, if you can and the person welcomes your help. Also help the person assess whether the option worked. If not, ask what's the next option to pursue, besides suicide?

The problem-solving method gives you a way to connect with your loved one in their struggle. You're on the same team, after all, and you can work together to find ways to ease the person's pain and problems.

Promote Pleasure

Sitting by a fire, petting a dog, eating a chocolate bar, taking a walk in nature—whatever can give people pleasure or, at least, distract them—might seem small in the face of overwhelming problems. The relief can't last long. But it can last moments, and just a few moments of pleasure can set off a chain reaction that broadens one's perspective and creates space for more positive emotions to follow. The psychologist Barbara Fredrickson (2009) calls this an "upward spiral," in contrast to the downward spiral of despair.

Some people may struggle to come up with things they enjoy. You can help, by asking various questions:

- "What can you do today for just a few moments of pleasure, even if it's as simple as eating your favorite food or watching a funny TV show?"

- "What do you do for fun?"

- "What things did you like to do as a child? Could you do one of those for just a few minutes today?"

Assure the person you don't expect whatever small thing they do to solve all their problems and cure them of suicidal thoughts. You just want them to experience at least a few moments of pleasure so that, perhaps someday soon, more can come.

Share Stories of Recovery

Ken Baldwin jumped off the Golden Gate Bridge in 1985, when he was twenty-eight years old. Baldwin told a reporter that once he became airborne, "I instantly realized that everything in my life that I'd thought was unfixable was totally fixable—except for having just jumped" (Friend 2003). Shannon Parkin intentionally stepped in front of a Metro train in Maryland in 2015. Although both her feet were partly amputated as a result, she wrote six years later, "I know I live with depression. Despite this illness, I have also been given gifts… I am grateful that I'm alive" (Parkin 2021).

Obviously, one person's epiphany doesn't mean everyone will rediscover the will to live. But these accounts reveal the power of suicidal thinking to distort facts and drown out hope. They also testify to the power of possibilities. For some people, others' experiences can serve as a postcard from the landscape outside of hell.

If someone you love thinks of suicide, there's hope. You know why? Because the person is still alive. I know, it's such a cliché—*where there is life, there is hope*—but if you dive beneath the surface of the words, you find truth. Something has kept your loved one alive, so far. Together, you can search for what those reasons for living are, whether based on hope, fear, pleasure, purpose, or all of the above.

CHAPTER 12

Recovery and Suicidal Thoughts

As you near the end of this book, it's possible your loved one's suicidal thoughts are as strong now as when you started reading the introduction and you fear the person won't survive. Or maybe the person no longer considers suicide an option and you fear they'll change their mind. The unknowns are uncomfortable in both directions: Will suicidal thoughts ever leave? Will they ever return? This chapter gives you a realistic picture of the different pathways people can take out of suicidal danger, what helps them get there, and the growth that can come in the process—not only for the person you love but for you, too.

What does it mean to recover from suicidal thoughts? The ideal, of course, is for the person you love to stop thinking of suicide. Fortunately, this ideal often is realized. Researchers interviewed hundreds of people who disclosed they'd ever seriously considered suicide. Those same people were interviewed again ten years later. In the intervening decade, two-thirds had no suicidal thoughts or attempts (Borges et al. 2008).

It's wonderful that suicidal thoughts completely left for two-thirds of people. But what about the other third who still, or again, had suicidal thoughts? Does that mean they didn't recover, too? Not necessarily.

People who continue to have suicidal thoughts, whether occasionally or persistently, can make life-saving progress in other ways. They might:

- Learn to observe suicidal thoughts as momentary events of the mind, like a storm, that need not be acted on

- Regard their suicidal thoughts as a symptom that they need to make a change, in the same way that hunger pangs alert us to eat

- Develop coping skills to better manage their suicidal thoughts and other problems

- Experience joy, pleasure, hope, and relaxation more often

- Feel a greater sense of purpose and meaning in life, which sustains them in difficult times

- Maintain hope they'll get through this hard time, just as they've survived all the others

- Turn more easily to friends, family, and mental health professionals for help

- Believe that life is worth living, in spite of the pain and problems that come with it

Recovery is relative. Some people, tragically, don't get better. They end their life. Still, when two-thirds of people with a history of suicidal thoughts or behavior go a decade without experiencing them again, and many others learn to successfully manage their recurring suicidal thoughts, that's cause for hope.

Here are some examples of the different forms recovery can take:

Jackson, seventeen, never had emotional problems until his sophomore year of high school. He couldn't pinpoint the cause, but he often felt down on himself. When he started fantasizing about shooting himself with his hunting rifle, it scared him. He told his parents and they took him to his pediatrician the next day. The physician diagnosed him with depression and prescribed an antidepressant. She warned Jackson and his parents that antidepressants can paradoxically increase suicidal thoughts, but she said untreated depression can pose an even greater hazard. Jackson agreed to try the medication, in combination with psychotherapy.

Within weeks, Jackson's sleep improved. This seemed to set off a chain reaction. Better rested, he could think more clearly. Better able to think, he felt less down on himself. Soon, his suicidal thoughts subsided. He continued with psychotherapy so he could understand better what had happened, and what to do if it happened again.

Rebecca experiences suicidal thoughts whenever her bipolar disorder causes yet another depressive episode. When this first happened, she believed everything she thought. "I should kill myself" meant, literally, she should kill herself. She attempted suicide at twenty-three, and that's what led her to first start therapy and medication.

Therapy helped Rebecca regard her suicidal thoughts as a sign something's gone awry. "I try to stay curious about why my mind has turned to suicide, and what it means I need right now," Rebecca says. "Sometimes, it's just a long night's sleep or time in nature, but other times it's a change in medication or more intensive therapy. I used to think of all the ways I could kill myself. Now, when suicidal thoughts come, I think of what I need to do to feel better."

Demetri first thought of suicide as a young child. Decades later at forty-four, he still thinks sometimes of killing himself. His therapist helped him recognize his mind had developed a cognitive habit: when he's in distress, his mind goes to suicide as an option, which helps him to feel less trapped. His mind has learned how to get relief. Now that Demetri recognizes why his mind turns so easily to suicide, he takes the thoughts less seriously.

"I know my brain's trying to help me, in a warped way," Demetri says. "It's just doing what it's done for so many years, but I don't need to listen to it."

What Helps People Recover?

Some people just wake up one day and feel better. Others trudge for months, even years, through feelings of hopelessness and a longing to die. Some never have suicidal thoughts again, and some never stop thinking of suicide. Still, even with the variety of experiences, stories of recovery tend to share the following ingredients (Chan et al. 2017).

A Turning Point

First, something happens that makes the person realize they want, at least a little, to stay alive. This "turning point" could be psychiatric hospitalization or other professional help; a change in a toxic relationship, job, or living situation; or a visceral, new understanding of the harm one's suicide would do to others (Chan et al. 2017).

Healthy Coping Skills

Learning new ways to cope with stress, trauma, and psychological pain can help weaken suicide's allure. These are just some of the habits people might adopt, or increase, on their path to recovery:

- Journaling

- Exercise

- Creative arts

- Mindfulness

- Yoga

- Self-help books

- Better self-care (e.g., healthy eating, regular sleep)

- Talking with others about problems

- Religion or spirituality

Supportive Connections

People who successfully moved through suicidal crises consistently report other people helped them. These can include loved ones like you, as well as mental health professionals, peer-support workers, a religious community, and more. This is only one reason why you have such a valuable role to play in helping your loved one not only to stay safe and alive but also to thrive.

Goals, Purpose, and Meaning

Remember how the philosopher Friedrich Nietzsche (2012) said the thought of suicide helps many people get through a difficult night? Nietzsche (1998) said something else relevant, too: "If you have your *why?* for life you can bear almost any *how?*" Many people who recover from suicidal thoughts discover—or make—meaning in their experiences, even the painful ones. They have a sense of purpose—goals to achieve, things to learn, people to help and love.

Self-Acceptance

Easing self-blame and self-criticism can be transformative. One person in the study by Chan et al. (2017, 362) wrote, "I realized that I am a very good person who for some reason had had bad experiences that I did not provoke, and in some point I could not control."

And More

Many other changes can lead to healing. Challenging unrealistic thought patterns. Rediscovering hope. Breaking out of the constricted tunnel vision that accompanies suicidality. Receiving evidence-based therapy. Trying a new medication. There are many pathways to recovery.

For people already out of the danger zone, it's not guaranteed they'll stay there. Of course, this is true of everybody, suicidal or not: it's impossible to know who will and who won't have thoughts one day of ending their life. If your loved one's suicidal thoughts have departed, you can help the person prepare for the possibility of relapse—*just in case.*

First, it's good to help your loved one consider what they've learned from the ordeal. If the person magically relived the situation, what skills could they use now that they didn't know earlier? What kind of situation might make the person vulnerable to suicidal thoughts coming back? What will the person do if that happens? These are the kinds of questions that get asked as part of a relapse prevention plan in cognitive therapy for suicide prevention (Wenzel et al. 2009).

If the person you care about completes a relapse prevention plan in therapy, ask what it involves. Ask what you can do to help, too, if that feels appropriate.

If your loved one isn't in therapy or doesn't do a relapse prevention plan there, you can have an informal conversation about the same topics. Invite them to describe in detail the steps they'll take if suicidal thoughts return, both as a way to etch these ideas into their memory and to edify you. You can also propose a recovery plan.

A Recovery Plan

A recovery plan is similar to a safety plan (chapter 7), but with one crucial difference: A safety plan focuses on survival. A recovery plan focuses on getting—and staying—better. One option is the Wellness Recovery and Action Plan, called a WRAP (Copeland 2010). It's designed for anybody who faces challenges with mental health, not only suicidal thoughts. A WRAP contains many different components:

Wellness Toolbox

For this, people create a list of things they can do to feel even just a little relief, hope, or satisfaction. The overriding question for someone to ask is, "What helps me feel better?" The longer the list, the better; a list several pages long isn't uncommon. Nothing is too big or too small. Common activities include (Copeland 2010):

- Brush my teeth

- Text a friend

- Take a bath or shower

- Brew my favorite coffee

- Get more sleep

- Play video games

- Listen to music

- Walk in nature

- Pet my cat or dog

- See my therapist, psychiatrist, or other doctor

Daily Maintenance

Here, the person makes lists of different things they need to do every day to stay well. Typically, the maintenance plan draws from activities already listed in the person's wellness toolbox—like eating healthfully, exercising, maintaining a daily routine, and keeping a regular sleep schedule—but the possibilities are limitless.

Triggers

Generally, as part of their WRAP, people identify events and circumstances that lead to distress, such as anger, sadness, and anxiety. Triggers could include criticism from a boss, an argument with a partner or parent, a poor grade on an exam—just about anything, really, depending on the person.

Early Warning Signs

Whereas triggers represent external events and circumstances, warning signs in the recovery plan are internal. The person identifies thoughts, feelings, behaviors, moods, physical symptoms, and other patterns (e.g., forgetting things more often or repeatedly waking up in the middle of the night) that signal potential trouble ahead. Once again, after identifying these warning signs, the person selects activities from their wellness toolbox to try to feel better and prevent the situation from deteriorating.

When Things Are Breaking Down

Up until now, the WRAP has been preventative. Now it looks at what to do when a crisis begins. The list of steps to take should be relatively brief, to avoid overwhelm in a vulnerable state. Examples might include making an emergency appointment with one's psychiatrist or therapist, staying with a friend to avoid being alone, and taking sick days at work.

Crisis Plan

The crisis plan is like an advance directive; it makes clear what actions the person wants others to take in case the person becomes so depressed, psychotic, or otherwise impaired that they can't make rational decisions. The person writes down people they want to help them, treatments that have helped—and *not* helped—in the past, unacceptable and acceptable treatment facilities, and other details like special instructions for tending to their pets and plants.

Post-Crisis Plan

As with other sections of the WRAP, the post-crisis plan is very practical. It lists people to support the person, things others can do to help, tasks that must be attended to and those that can wait, and signs that the crisis has subsided, at which point the person returns to their daily maintenance plan.

Obviously, creating a WRAP takes a lot of time and thought. It's sort of a safety plan on steroids. In many cities, a community mental health agency holds classes or peer-support groups to help people create a WRAP. To learn more, see https://www.wellnessrecoveryactionplan .com or the book *WRAP Plus* by Mary Ellen Copeland (2010).

Post-Traumatic Growth

No matter where you and your loved one are in the process—whether in crisis, a chronic state of stress, or recovery—you've endured a life-changing event. You've gone through it together in one sense, but also separately, with different needs, hopes, and fears. In what ways has this experience changed you? Consider both negative and positive changes. Because, yes, sometimes good things come out of harrowing ordeals.

It might offend you for me to suggest there could be a "bright side" to a loved one's suicidality. No doubt, the experience is difficult in many ways. At the same time, unexpected changes can occur—for the better—as a result.

In your journal, write down which of the following statements is true for you in your experience of loving someone with suicidal thoughts.

- I have a greater appreciation for the people I love.

- My empathy for my loved one has increased.

- I listen better than I used to.

- I feel closer to the person I love as a result of knowing what they're going through.

- My religious or spiritual faith has deepened.

- I express love, care, and concern more.

- I feel more compassion toward myself and others.

- I feel gratitude for things I used to take for granted.

- My sense of purpose and meaning in life is stronger.

- I have a clearer perspective now on what's important and what's not in life.

- It feels good to help and support the person I love.

- I've learned a lot about mental illness, stress, and suicidality.

- I'm better able to help friends and family with mental health challenges.

- This experience has helped me discover my strengths.

- I'm better able to initiate conversations about tough topics.

- I'm more open to asking for help.

- I've discovered my friends and family will truly be there for me.

- I take better care of myself physically and mentally.

You might not relate to many of these sentiments now, or even later. People heal at their own pace. If any statements do apply to you, I recommend writing in your journal what you'll do with this knowledge moving forward. Even amid all the pain, all the turmoil, and all the loss, have you gained anything that you wouldn't want to give up?

Closing Thoughts

Your reading this book has been an act of love. You're trying to learn as much as you can to help someone you love who has suicidal thoughts. And you learned in these pages ways to take care of your needs, too. What are the most important things you learned? What will you do differently as a result? Write it all down in your journal, both to process the past and, perhaps, to give advice to your future self, in case you need it.

I truly hope the person you love stays safe and well. I hope you do, too. Feel free to drop me a line at my website, Speaking of Suicide (https://www.speakingofsuicide.com), if you wish. I'd love to hear from you.

There's a saying I like: "If you're going through hell, keep going." May you and everybody you love keep going.

Acknowledgments

To my psychotherapy clients, readers of my website, and others who have shared their challenges of loving someone with suicidal thoughts; to my mother, Beverly Freedenthal, who experienced these challenges with me, years ago; to my husband, Pete, for his support, love, and luscious meals, along with many conversations about this book; to our son, Ian, for permitting me to share his story; to my coach, Beth Vagle, for her usual brilliance and good cheer; to my friend Jenny-Lynn Ellis for her support through the writing process; to my friend Lena Heilmann, for her late-night texts about the book; to my colleagues John Draper, PhD, and David Jobes, PhD, for reviewing portions of the manuscript; to Amanda Moore McBride, PhD, dean of the University of Denver Graduate School of Social Work, whose support of my writing has been unwavering; to Wendy Millstine, acquisitions editor at New Harbinger, who reached out to me about writing this book and guided me through the proposal process; to my editors Jennye Garibaldi and Jennifer Holder, for their patience and acumen thereafter; to Caveday, for providing a reliable structure online for showing up to do the writing; and to anyone else who helped bring this book to fruition, thank you.

Resources

Some of the following resources are for people with suicidal thoughts, and most are also for the people who love them.

Hotlines

United States

988 Suicide & Crisis Lifeline
(https://988lifeline.org)
   Trained counselors are available by phone or chat 24/7. Call if you—or someone you're concerned about—are thinking about suicide or otherwise need psychological support.

- 988: This is a shortcut to reach the 988 Suicide & Crisis Lifeline.

- 800-273-8255: Full number for the 988 Suicide & Crisis Lifeline

- 888-628-9454: Spanish

- 711 + 800-273-8255: For people who are deaf or hard of hearing, or they can use their preferred relay service

- To reach the chat service, go to https://988lifeline.org/chat/

Veterans Crisis Line: 988 or 800-273-8255, Press 1
(https://www.veteranscrisisline.net)

Crisis Text Line: Text "HOME" to 741741
(https://www.crisistextline.org)

Trans Lifeline's Hotline: 1-877-565-8860 (https://translifeline.org/)

Trevor Project Hotline: Phone 866-488-7386

- Text "START" to 678678

- Chat: Use the link at https://www.thetrevorproject.org
  /get-help/.

International

The following sites maintain directories of suicide hotlines around the world:

- Befrienders Worldwide: https://www.befrienders.org
  /need-to-talk

- Find a Helpline: https://findahelpline.com

For General Information and Advice About Suicide Prevention

American Foundation for Suicide Prevention: https://afsp.org

International Association for Suicide Prevention:
https://www.iasp.info/

Speaking of Suicide: https://www.speakingofsuicide.com

This site, created by the book's author, has articles and resources for everyone touched by suicidality in some way, including individuals with suicidal thoughts and their family, friends, and partners, suicide attempt survivors, suicide loss survivors—"and others who care."

Peer Support for Individuals with Suicidal Thoughts

The following sites' guidelines do not permit encouraging suicide or providing explicit instructions on how to die by suicide.

Chronic Suicide Support: https://www.chronicsuicidesupport.com

You'll find here a forum for people who want to talk about their long-standing suicidal thoughts with others who have similar experiences.

r/SuicideWatch: https://www.reddit.com/r/SuicideWatch/

Billed as "peer support for anyone with suicidal thoughts," this site had 370,000 members as of August 2022. The site is also useful for family, friends, and partners who want to better understand different suicidal experiences.

Recovery Stories

Live Through This: https://www.livethroughthis.org

This website features photographic portraits and in-depth interviews with people who tried to end their life. These aren't always feel-good stories where everyone lives happily ever after, but you can see how people of diverse ages, races, and backgrounds cope, grow, and change as they live through this. Dese'Rae L. Stage, herself a suicide attempt survivor, created the site.

Stories of Hope and Recovery: https://988lifeline.org/stories/

This site, part of the National Suicide Prevention Lifeline, offers carefully curated, inspirational stories and videos from sites such as The Mighty, Hope Inc., The American Foundation for Suicide Prevention, and more.

Books for Individuals with Suicidal Thoughts

The Suicidal Thoughts Workbook: CBT Skills to Reduce Emotional Pain, Increase Hope, and Prevent Suicide (Gordon 2021)

How I Stayed Alive when My Brain Was Trying to Kill Me: One Person's Guide to Suicide Prevention (Blauner 2002)

Choosing to Live: How to Defeat Suicide Through Cognitive Therapy (Ellis and Newman 1996)

References

American Psychiatric Association. 2022. *Diagnostic and Statistical Manual of Mental Disorders (5th Ed. Text Revision)*: *DSM-5-TR*. Washington, DC: American Psychiatric Association.

Anderson, K. J. 2010. *Life, in Spite of Me*. Colorado Springs, CO: Multnomah Books.

Anglemyer, A., T. Horvath, and G. Rutherford. 2014. "The Accessibility of Firearms and Risk for Suicide and Homicide Victimization Among Household Members: A Systematic Review and Meta-Analysis." *Annals of Internal Medicine* 160: 101–110.

Beck, J. 2021. *Cognitive Behavior Therapy: Basics and Beyond (3rd Edition)*. New York: Guilford.

Benson, H. and W. Proctor. 2011. *Relaxation Revolution: The Science and Genetics of Mind Body Healing*. New York: Simon and Schuster.

Blades, C. A., W. G. Stritzke, A. C. Page, and J. D. Brown. 2018. "The Benefits and Risks of Asking Research Participants About Suicide: A Meta-Analysis of the Impact of Exposure to Suicide-Related Content." *Clinical Psychology Review* 64: 1–12.

Blauner, S. R. 2002. *How I Stayed Alive When My Brain Was Trying to Kill Me: One Person's Guide to Suicide Prevention*. New York: Harper Collins.

Borges, G., J. Angst, M. K. Nock, A. M. Ruscio, and R. C. Kessler. 2008. "Risk Factors for the Incidence and Persistence of Suicide-Related Outcomes: A 10-Year Follow-up Study Using the National Comorbidity Surveys." *Journal of Affective Disorders* 105: 25–33.

Bostwick, J. M. and V. S. Pankratz. 2000. "Affective Disorders and Suicide Risk: A Reexamination." *American Journal of Psychiatry* 157: 1925–1932.

Calati, R. and P. Courtet. 2016. "Is Psychotherapy Effective for Reducing Suicide Attempt and Non-Suicidal Self-Injury Rates? Meta-Analysis and Meta-Regression of Literature Data." *Journal of Psychiatric Research* 79: 8–20.

Chamberlain, S. 2012. "Narrative Therapy: Challenges and Communities of Practice." In *Discursive Perspectives in Therapeutic Practice*, edited by A. Lock and T. Strong. Oxford: Oxford University Press.

Chan, K. J., H. Kirkpatrick, and J. Brasch. 2017. "The Reasons to Go on Living Project: Stories of Recovery After a Suicide Attempt." *Qualitative Research in Psychology* 14: 350–373.

Chung, D., D. Hadzi-Pavlovic, M. Wang, S. Swaraj, M. Olfson, and M. Large. 2019. "Meta-Analysis of Suicide Rates in the First Week and the First Month After Psychiatric Hospitalisation." *BMJ Open* 9: e023883.

Copeland, M. E. 2010. *WRAP Plus*. Dummerston, VT: Peach Press.

Davis, M., E. R. Eshelman, and M. McKay. 2019. *The Relaxation and Stress Reduction Workbook (7th Ed.)*. Oakland, CA: New Harbinger Publications.

DeCou, C. R. and M. E. Schumann. 2018. "On the Iatrogenic Risk of Assessing Suicidality: A Meta-Analysis." *Suicide and Life-Threatening Behavior* 48: 531–543.

Dembosky, A. November 28, 2021. "Americans Can Wait Many Weeks to See a Therapist. California Law Aims to Fix That." National Public Radio, https://www.npr.org/sections/health-shots/2021/11/18/1053566020 /americans-can-wait-many-weeks-to-see-a-therapist-california-law-aims -to-fix-that.

Demesmaeker, A., E. Chazard, A. Hoang, G. Vaiva, and A. Amad. 2022. "Suicide Mortality After a Nonfatal Suicide Attempt: A Systematic Review and Meta-Analysis." *Australian and New Zealand Journal of Psychiatry* 56: 603–616.

Downie, J., M. Gupta, S. Cavalli, and S. Blouin. 2022. "Assistance in Dying: A Comparative Look at Legal Definitions." *Death Studies* 46: 1547–1556.

Doyle, K. September 22, 2020. "Suicide and Mortal Sin: What Is True Forgiveness?" *The Catholic Review*. https://catholicreview.org/suicide-and-mortal -sin-what-is-true-forgiveness/.

Edwards, F., H. Lee, and M. Esposito. 2019. "Risk of Being Killed by Police Use of Force in the United States by Age, Race–Ethnicity, and Sex." *Proceedings of the National Academy of Sciences* 116: 16793–16798.

Ellis, T. E. and C. F. Newman. 1996. *Choosing to Live: How to Defeat Suicide Through Cognitive Therapy*. Oakland, CA: New Harbinger Publications.

Ellis, T. E. 2006. *Cognition and Suicide: Theory, Research, and Therapy*. Washington, DC: American Psychological Association.

Faber, A. and E. Mazlish. 2012. *How to Talk so Kids Will Listen & Listen so Kids Will Talk*. New York: Scribner.

Ferguson, M., K. Rhodes, M. Loughhead, H. McIntyre, and N. Procter. 2021. "The Effectiveness of the Safety Planning Intervention for Adults Experiencing Suicide-Related Distress: A Systematic Review." *Archives of Suicide Research* 1–24.

Fornaro, M., A. Anastasia, A. Valchera, A. Carano, L. Orsolini, F. Vellante, G. Rapini, et al. 2019. "The FDA 'Black Box' Warning on Antidepressant Suicide Risk in Young Adults: More Harm Than Benefits?" *Frontiers in Psychiatry* 10: 294–294.

Foster Wallace, D. 1996. *Infinite Jest.* New York: Little, Brown, and Company.

Frankham, E. 2018. "Mental Illness Affects Police Fatal Shootings." *Contexts* 17: 70–72.

Fredrickson, B. 2009. *Positivity: Discover the Upward Spiral That Will Change Your Life.* New York: Harmony.

Freedenthal, S. 2018. *Helping the Suicidal Person: Tips and Techniques for Professionals.* New York: Routledge.

Frey, L. M., Q. A. Hunt, J. M. Russon, and G. Diamond. 2022. "Review of Family-Based Treatments from 2010 to 2019 for Suicidal Ideation and Behavior." *Journal of Marital and Family Therapy* 48: 154–177.

Friend, T. October 13, 2003. "Jumpers: The Fatal Grandeur of the Golden Gate Bridge." *The New Yorker.*

Frost, H., P. Campbell, M. Maxwell, R. E. O'Carroll, S. U. Dombrowski, B. Williams, H. Cheyne, E. Coles, and A. Pollock. 2018. "Effectiveness of Motivational Interviewing on Adult Behaviour Change in Health and Social Care Settings: A Systematic Review of Reviews." *PloS One* 13: e0204890.

Gordon, K. H. 2021. *The Suicidal Thoughts Workbook: CBT Skills to Reduce Emotional Pain, Increase Hope, and Prevent Suicide.* Oakland, CA: New Harbinger Publications.

Greene, G. 2015. *The Power and the Glory.* New York: Penguin Press.

Gvion, Y., H. Rozett, and T. Stern. 2020. "Will You Agree to Treat a Suicidal Adolescent? A Comparative Study Among Mental Health Professionals." *European Child and Adolescent Psychiatry* 30: 671–680.

Hanh, T. N. 1987. *The Miracle of Mindfulness: An Introduction to the Practice of Meditation:* Boston: Beacon Press.

Hawkins, E. M., W. Coryell, S. Leung, S. V. Parikh, C. Weston, P. Nestadt, J. I. Nurnberger Jr., et al. 2021. "Effects of Somatic Treatments on Suicidal Ideation and Completed Suicides." *Brain and Behavior* 11: e2381.

Hawton, K., E. Townsend, J. Deeks, L. Appleby, D. Gunnel, O. Bennewith, and J. Cooper. 2001. "Effects of Legislation Restricting Pack Sizes of Paracetamol and Salicylate on Self Poisoning in the United Kingdom: Before and After Study." *British Medical Journal* 322: 1–7.

Hay, J. October 10, 2015. "Kevin Briggs Reflects on 18 Years of Stopping Golden Gate Bridge Suicides." *The Press Democrat,* https://www.pressdemocrat.com /article/news/kevin-briggs-reflects-on-18-years-of-stopping-golden-gate -bridge-suicides/.

Hayes, S. C. and S. Smith. 2005. *Get out of Your Mind and into Your Life: The New Acceptance and Commitment Therapy.* Oakland, CA: New Harbinger Publications.

Hengartner, M. P., S. Amendola, J. A. Kaminski, S. Kindler, T. Bschor, and M. Plöderl. 2021. "Suicide Risk with Selective Serotonin Reuptake Inhibitors and Other New-Generation Antidepressants in Adults: A Systematic Review and Meta-Analysis of Observational Studies." *Journal of Epidemiology and Community Health* 75: 523–530.

Hetrick, S. E., J. E. McKenzie, A. P. Bailey, V. Sharma, C. I. Moller, P. B. Badcock, G. R. Cox, S. N. Merry, and N. Meader. 2021. "New Generation Antidepressants for Depression in Children and Adolescents: A Network Meta-Analysis." *Cochrane Database of Systematic Reviews.*

Holmstrand, C., M. Bogren, C. Mattisson, and L. Brådvik. 2015. "Long-Term Suicide Risk in No, One or More Mental Disorders: The Lundby Study 1947–1997." *Acta Psychiatrica Scandinavica* 132: 459–469.

Hom, M. A., I. H. Stanley, M. C. Podlogar, and T. E. Joiner. 2017. "'Are You Having Thoughts of Suicide?': Examining Experiences with Disclosing and Denying Suicidal Ideation." *Journal of Clinical Psychology* 73: 1382–1392.

Hope Inc. Stories. April 12, 2021. *Not Just a White Thing: Moving America's Soul on Suicide—Ep. 2.* YouTube. https://youtu.be/V46LJLwhVIw.

Hummel, C. 1994. *Priorities: Tyranny of the Urgent.* Downers Grove, IL: InterVarsity Press.

Hunter, J., R. Maunder, P. Kurdyak, A. S. Wilton, A. Gruneir, and S. Vigod. 2018. "Mental Health Follow-up After Deliberate Self-Harm and Risk for Repeat Self-Harm and Death." *Psychiatry Research* 259: 333–339.

Ivey-Stephenson, A. Z., Z. Demissie, A. E. Crosby, D. M. Stone, E. Gaylor, N. Wilkins, R. Lowry, and M. Brown. 2020. "Suicidal Ideation and Behaviors Among High School Students: Youth Risk Behavior Survey, United States, 2019." *MMWR Supplements* 69: 47–55.

Jeffers, S. 1987. *Feel the Fear and Do It Anyway.* San Diego, CA: Harcourt Brace Jovanovich.

Jones, J. D., R. C. Boyd, M. E. Calkins, A. Ahmed, T. M. Moore, R. Barzilay, T. D. Benton, and R. E. Gur. 2019. "Parent-Adolescent Agreement About Adolescents' Suicidal Thoughts." *Pediatrics* 143: e20181771.

Jordan, J. R. and J. L. McIntosh. 2011. "Is Suicide Bereavement Different?: Perspectives from Research and Practice." In *Grief and Bereavement in Contemporary Society,* edited by R. A. Neimeyer, D. L. Harris, H. R. Winokuer, and G. F. Thornton. New York: Routledge.

214

Kamenov, K., C. Twomey, M. Cabello, A. M. Prina, and J. L. Ayuso-Mateos. 2017. "The Efficacy of Psychotherapy, Pharmacotherapy and Their Combination on Functioning and Quality of Life in Depression: A Meta-Analysis." *Psychological Medicine* 47: 414–425.

Kauffman, J. 2013. *Loss of the Assumptive World: A Theory of Traumatic Loss.* New York: Routledge.

Kessler, R. C., P. Berglund, G. Borges, M. Nock, and P. S. Wang. 2005. "Trends in Suicide Ideation, Plans, Gestures, and Attempts in the United States, 1990–1992 to 2001–2003." *Journal of the American Medical Association* 293: 2487–2495.

King, F. 2017. "A Matter of Laugh or Death." Filmed at TEDxRenfrewCollingwood, 19:10, https://youtu.be/aBUXND5BD4M.

Kübler-Ross, E. and D. Kessler. 2005. *On Grief and Grieving: Finding the Meaning of Grief Through the Five Stages of Loss.* New York: Simon and Schuster.

Labouliere, C. D., K. L. Green, P. Vasan, A. Cummings, D. Layman, J. Kammer, M. Rahman, et al. 2021. "Is the Outpatient Mental Health Workforce Ready to Save Lives? Suicide Prevention Training, Knowledge, Self-Efficacy, and Clinical Practices Prior to the Implementation of a Statewide Suicide Prevention Initiative." *Suicide and Life-Threatening Behavior* 51: 325–333.

Levi-Belz, Y., T. Gavish-Marom, S. Barzilay, A. Apter, V. Carli, C. Hoven, M. Sarchiapone, and D. Wasserman. 2019. "Psychosocial Factors Correlated with Undisclosed Suicide Attempts to Significant Others: Findings from the Adolescence SEYLE Study." *Suicide and Life-Threatening Behavior* 49: 759–773.

Liu, B. P., K. B. Lunde, C.-X. Jia, and P. Qin. 2020. "The Short-Term Rate of Non-Fatal and Fatal Repetition of Deliberate Self-Harm: A Systematic Review and Meta-Analysis of Longitudinal Studies." *Journal of Affective Disorders* 273: 597–603.

Macrynikola, N., E. Auad, J. Menjivar, and R. Miranda. 2021. "Does Social Media Use Confer Suicide Risk? A Systematic Review of the Evidence." *Computers in Human Behavior Reports* 3: 100094.

Mason, A., K. Jang, K. Morley, D. Scarf, S. C. Collings, and B. C. Riordan. 2021. "A Content Analysis of Reddit Users' Perspectives on Reasons for Not Following Through with a Suicide Attempt." *Cyberpsychology, Behavior, and Social Networking* 24: 642–647.

Méndez-Bustos, P., R. Calati, F. Rubio-Ramírez, E. Olié, P. Courtet, and J. Lopez-Castroman. 2019. "Effectiveness of Psychotherapy on Suicidal Risk: A Systematic Review of Observational Studies." *Frontiers in Psychology* 10: 277.

Miller, W. R. and S. Rollnick. 2004. "Talking Oneself into Change: Motivational Interviewing, Stages of Change, and Therapeutic Process." *Journal of Cognitive Psychotherapy* 18: 299–308.

Miller, W. R. and S. Rollnick. 2013. *Motivational Interviewing: Helping People Change (3rd Ed.)*. New York: Guilford.

Milner, A., J. Sveticic, and D. D. Leo. 2013. "Suicide in the Absence of Mental Disorder? A Review of Psychological Autopsy Studies Across Countries." *International Journal of Social Psychiatry* 59: 545–554.

Mishara, B. L. 1999. "Conceptions of Death and Suicide in Children Ages 6–12 and Their Implications for Suicide Prevention." *Suicide and Life-Threatening Behavior* 29: 105–118.

Moitra, M., D. Santomauro, L. Degenhardt, P. Y. Collins, H. Whiteford, T. Vos, and A. Ferrari. 2021. "Estimating the Risk of Suicide Associated with Mental Disorders: A Systematic Review and Meta-Regression Analysis." *Journal of Psychiatric Research* 137: 242–249.

Monteiro, G. (2002). " 'Stopping by Woods,' Once Again." *The Robert Frost Review* 12: 66–68.

Myers, M. F. and C. Fine. 2006. *Touched by Suicide: Hope and Healing after Loss*. New York: Penguin.

Neff, K. 2011. *Self-Compassion: The Proven Power of Being Kind to Yourself*. New York: Harper Collins.

Nezu, A. M., A. P. Greenfield, and C. M. Nezu. 2015. "Contemporary Problem-Solving Therapy: A Transdiagnostic Intervention." In *The Oxford Handbook of Cognitive and Behavioral Therapies*, edited by C. M. Nezu and A. M. Nezu. New York: Oxford University Press.

Nietzsche, F. W. 1998. *Twilight of the Idols*. Translated by D. Large. Oxford: Oxford University Press.

Nietzsche, F. W. 2012. *Beyond Good and Evil*. Translated by H. Zimmern. Andrews UK Limited.

Norman, S., C. Allard, K. Browne, C. Capone, B. Davis, and E. Kubany. 2019. *Trauma Informed Guilt Reduction Therapy: Treating Guilt and Shame Resulting from Trauma and Moral Injury*. London: Academic Press.

Nuij, C., W. van Ballegooijen, D. de Beurs, D. Juniar, A. Erlangsen, G. Portzky, R. C. O'Connor, et al. 2021. "Safety Planning-Type Interventions for Suicide Prevention: Meta-Analysis." *British Journal of Psychiatry* 219: 419–426.

O'Keeffe, S., M. Suzuki, M. Ryan, J. Hunter, and R. McCabe. 2021. "Experiences of Care for Self-Harm in the Emergency Department: Comparison of the Perspectives of Patients, Carers and Practitioners." *BJPsych Open* 7: E175.

Oettingen, G. 2015. *Rethinking Positive Thinking: Inside the New Science of Motivation*. New York: Penguin.

Ott, M. J. 2004. "Mindfulness Meditation: A Path of Transformation & Healing." *Journal of Psychosocial Nursing and Mental Health Services* 42: 22–29.

Owens, P. L., K. R. Fingar, K. W. McDermott, P. K. Muhuri, and K. C. Heslin. 2019. *Statistical Brief #249: Inpatient Stays Involving Mental and Substance Use Disorders, 2016*. Rockville, MD: U.S. Agency for Healthcare Research and Quality.

Paashaus, L., T. Forkmann, H. Glaesmer, G. Juckel, D. Rath, A. Schönfelder, and T. Teismann. 2021. "From Decision to Action: Suicidal History and Time Between Decision to Die and Actual Suicide Attempt." *Clinical Psychology & Psychotherapy* 28:1427–1434.

Parkin, S. H. April 15, 2021. "Embracing Hope Through Six-Foot Balloons." *Please See Me*. https://pleaseseeme.com/issue-7/nonfiction/embracing-hope -through-six-foot-balloons-shannon-heath-parkin/.

Phillips, J. G. and L. Mann. 2019. "Suicide Baiting in the Internet Era." *Computers in Human Behavior* 92: 29–36.

Polihronis, C., P. Cloutier, J. Kaur, R. Skinner, and M. Cappelli. 2020. "What's the Harm in Asking? A Systematic Review and Meta-Analysis on the Risks of Asking About Suicide-Related Behaviors and Self-Harm with Quality Appraisal." *Archives of Suicide Research* 1–23.

Pompili, M., M. B. Murri, S. Patti, M. Innamorati, D. Lester, P. Girardi, and M. Amore. 2016. "The Communication of Suicidal Intentions: A Meta-Analysis." *Psychological Medicine* 46: 2239–2253.

Quinnett, P. 2019. "The Role of Clinician Fear in Interviewing Suicidal Patients." *Crisis* 40: 355–359.

Ralston, A. 2004. *Between a Rock and a Hard Place*. New York: Atria Books.

Roush, J. F., S. L. Brown, D. R. Jahn, S. M. Mitchell, N. J. Taylor, P. Quinnett, and R. Ries. 2018. "Mental Health Professionals' Suicide Risk Assessment and Management Practices." *Crisis* 39: 55–64.

Salhi, C., D. Azrael, and M. Miller. 2021. "Parent and Adolescent Reports of Adolescent Access to Household Firearms in the United States." *JAMA Network Open* 4: e210989.

Seiden, R. H. 1978. "Where Are They Now? A Follow-up Study of Suicide Attempters from the Golden Gate Bridge." *Suicide and Life-Threatening Behavior* 8: 203-216.

Shea, S. C. 1999. *The Practical Art of Suicide Assessment: A Guide for Mental Health Professionals and Substance Abuse Counselors*. New York: John Wiley.

Shneidman, E. S. 1996. *The Suicidal Mind*. Oxford: Oxford University Press.

Sidebotham, P. 2017. "Fatal Child Maltreatment." In *The Wiley Handbook of What Works in Child Maltreatment*, edited by L. Dixon, D. F. Perkins, C. Hamilton-Giachritsis, and L. A. Craig. Hoboken, NJ: John Wiley and Sons.

Siegel, A. N., J. D. Di Vincenzo, E. Brietzke, H. Gill, N. B. Rodrigues, L. M. Lui, K. M. Teopiz, et al. 2021. "Antisuicidal and Antidepressant Effects of Ketamine and Esketamine in Patients with Baseline Suicidal Ideation: A Systematic Review." *Journal of Psychiatric Research* 137: 426–436.

Simpson, J. 1988. *Touching the Void*. London: Jonathan Cape.

Simpson, S. A., R. Loh, C. R. Goans, K. Ryall, M. Middleton, and A. Dalton. 2021. "Suicide and Self-Harm Outcomes Among Psychiatric Emergency Service Patients Diagnosed as Malingering." *The Journal of Emergency Medicine* 61: 381–386.

Stone, D. M., T. R. Simon, K. A. Fowler, S. R. Kegler, K. Yuan, K. M. Holland, A. Z. Ivey-Stephenson, and A. E. Crosby. 2018. "Vital Signs: Trends in State Suicide Rates—United States, 1999–2016 and Circumstances Contributing to Suicide—27 States, 2015." *Morbidity and Mortality Weekly Report* 67: 617–624.

Substance Abuse and Mental Health Services Administration. 2020. *Key Substance Use and Mental Health Indicators in the United States: Results from the 2019 National Survey on Drug Use and Health*. Rockville, MD: Substance Abuse and Mental Health Services Administration.

Swisher, L. 2016. "Special Report: Emergency Physician, Mother, Suicide Risk." *Emergency Medicine News* 38: 10–11.

Tang, S., N. M. Reily, A. F. Arena, V. Sheanoda, J. Han, B. Draper, P. J. Batterham, A. J. Mackinnon, and H. Christensen. 2022. "Predictors of Not Receiving Mental Health Services Among People at Risk of Suicide: A Systematic Review." *Journal of Affective Disorders* 301: 172–188.

Verrocchio, M. C., D. Carrozzino, D. Marchetti, K. Andreasson, M. Fulcheri, and P. Bech. 2016. "Mental Pain and Suicide: A Systematic Review of the Literature." *Frontiers in Psychiatry* 7: 108.

Wang, D., M. S. Hagger, and N. L. Chatzisarantis. 2020. "Ironic Effects of Thought Suppression: A Meta-Analysis." *Perspectives on Psychological Science* 15: 778–793.

Wenzel, A., G. K. Brown, and A. T. Beck. 2009. *Cognitive Therapy for Suicidal Patients: Scientific and Clinical Applications*. Washington, DC: American Psychological Association.

Wenzel, A. and S. Jager-Hyman. 2012. "Cognitive Therapy for Suicidal Patients: Current Status." *The Behavior Therapist/AABT* 35: 121.

Zareian, B. and E. D. Klonsky. 2020. "Connectedness and Suicide." In *Alternatives to Suicide: Beyond Risk and Toward a Life Worth Living*, edited by A. C. Page and W. G. K. Stritzke. London: Academic Press.

Stacey Freedenthal, PhD, LCSW, is a psychotherapist and consultant in private practice in Denver, CO; and associate professor at the University of Denver Graduate School of Social Work. Freedenthal focuses her work on helping people who experience suicidal thoughts or behavior. She is author of *Helping the Suicidal Person: Tips and Techniques for Professionals*; and creator of the website, Speaking of Suicide.

Foreword writer **David A. Jobes, PhD**, is professor of psychology, associate director of clinical training, and director of the Suicide Prevention Laboratory at The Catholic University of America. He created the Collaborative Assessment and Management of Suicidality (CAMS), which is a suicide-focused clinical treatment supported by extensive clinical trial research. He is author of *Managing Suicidal Risk*.

MORE BOOKS from
NEW HARBINGER PUBLICATIONS

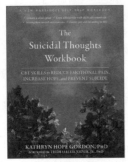

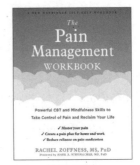

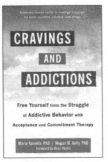
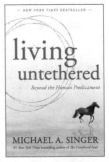